T H E

OVERNIGHT
JOB CHANGE
LETTER

M. Watkins

T H E
OVERNIGHT
JOB CHANGE
LETTER

Donald Asher

 Ten Speed Press

Ten Speed Press
P.O. Box 7123
Berkeley, California 94707

Text and cover design by Fifth Street Design, Berkeley, California

Library of Congress Cataloging-in-Publication Data

Asher, Donald.
    The Overnight Job Change Letter / Donald Asher
        p.   cm.
    Includes bibliographical references.
    ISBN 0-89815-595-9
    1. Cover letters. 2. Résumés (Employments). 3. Career changes.
4. Job hunting   I. Title.
HF5383.A838   1994
808′.0665—dc20   94-8321
                                                    CIP

FIRST PRINTING 1994

Printed in the United States of America

    2 3 4 5 — 98 97 96 95 94

A Note from the Author

The only significant difference between people who do things and people who don't is exactly that. Pick up this book and do something to make your life better.

— Donald Asher

Donald Asher, *President*
Résumé Righters
San Francisco
(415) 543-2020

Mailing Address:
Donald Asher
The Overnight Job Search Letter
c/o Ten Speed Press
P.O. Box 7123
Berkeley, California 94707

For Maureen Daly, who stole my heart with her mind.

Special thanks to Andrea Miskow, Kathy Priola, Kathleen Docherty, and Marsha Keeffer for running my business in my repeated absences. Special thanks as always to the wonderful crew at Ten Speed Press, Mariah, Phil, George, Christine, Leili, Chia-Ann, and Lisa. I couldn't have done it without you. A very special thanks to Danaelle Bell.

Some of the material in this book originally appeared in the *Wall Street Journal*'s *National Business Employment Weekly* and *Managing Your Career* magazines. These sections are used by permission of Dow Jones & Co., Inc. Some of this material also appeared in other forms in the companion titles to this book, *The Overnight Résumé* and *The Overnight Job Change Strategy,* and the chapter on letters of recommendation is adapted from a chapter in *Graduate Admissions Essays: What Works, What Doesn't, and Why.* These sections are adapted by permission of Ten Speed Press. My thanks to Ann Miya for the illustration on page 1, which is her copyright. Copyrighted cartoons are used by permission of the publishers. Alert readers will notice that this book has no chapter 13. It's intentional —I just wanted to do everything possible to bring you luck.

All of the letters in this book were written by or for real people, although many of the names, dates, and companies mentioned in the examples have been changed. No person mentioned in this book should be presumed to be any particular individual, and any such assumption would be unwarranted.

Job-Search Supply Cabinet

- 5 × 8-inch index cards to make lead cards

- 8½ × 11-inch stationery, for job-search letters: white, ivory, or light grey, 24-lb. minimum

- 7¼ × 10½-inch stationery for shorter but still formal job-search letters

- 5½ × 8½-inch or smaller stationery for handwritten notes

- Some formal thank-you cards, very conservative in style

- Résumés, customized for almost every mailing

- 9 × 12-inch envelopes in white or manila

- Business cards; make your own "jobseeker" cards

- Postage scale

- Answering machine or service, with formal outgoing message

- Fax capabilities, your own or easy access

- Word-processing capabilities, your own or easy access

- A coherent wardrobe, to the last detail

Contents

Preface
How to Use This Book

How to Get Started Fast

If you need a job-search letter by tomorrow morning, skip right now to chapter 2, "Components of Compelling Job-Search Letters," and follow the instructions as you go along. You will be able to craft a top-notch letter in less than an hour, even if you're not a natural writer. You can read the rest of the book another day.

If you have more time than that, keep reading straight through chapter 2, then read the chapter corresponding to the type of letter you need to write. For example, if you are writing a letter in response to a newspaper ad or other job announcement, you will want to read chapters 1, 2, and 3 ("Cover Letters for Announced Openings"). If you are writing a letter to a headhunter, you will want to read chapters 1, 2, and 6 ("Broadcast Letters for Headhunters"). Check the table of contents for other options. Unless you are seriously pressed for time, be sure to read chapter 1, "How People Get Jobs." If your letters are great but your strategy is not, then your job search may be a long one.

Some Assumptions About You, the Candidate

This book assumes that you have, at some point in your life, written at least one business letter. This frees me from having to warn you about every mistake you could ever possibly make. However, even if you have never written a letter before in your life, you will do fine if you just copy the "real-life" models in this book.

This book also makes the daring assumption that you are somebody special. There are too many books written for every possible candidate (the good, the bad, and the ugly); this book is tailored for strong performers like you. If you take a moment to think about it, I am sure that you will discover wonderful things about yourself that you could report to a potential employer. This book provides step-by-step job-hunting assistance, but if you come to the table with no idea of what you have to offer, you've got the wrong book. (If you *are* unsure of what you have to offer—or the type of job you want—there is no better book for you than *What Color is Your Parachute?* by Richard Bolles.)

The book in your hands is about *job-search* letters. You cannot conduct a job search without knowing what you want and what you have to offer. For this reason, letters seeking "informational interviews" are covered only briefly. If you want to know more about informational interviewing, read my book *From College to Career,* or Martha Stoodley's *Information Interviewing: What It Is and How to Use It in Your Career.* (See the Bibliography for these and other career titles of interest.)

Another daring assumption is that you are serious about your job search. Many of the best techniques in the book require you to be willing to make precise follow-up calls. If you are poorly organized, forgetful, and generally unable to follow through on your commitments, this might not be the best book for you. These techniques are hot, they're new, and I wouldn't want you to ruin them for anybody else. If you use this book you will be making promises in your cover letters. Be sure you are willing to deliver on those promises before you send each and every letter.

Finally, this book assumes that you are willing to look up words in the dictionary. The process of proofreading your work is mentioned only briefly, but it is most certainly your responsibility to send out letters that are perfect in grammar, spelling, and style. About half of the letter-and-résumé presentations I see contain an error of some sort. Do your best to make sure that your letter and résumé are error-free.

What This Book Offers

This book offers the most aggressive job-search letters you will find in any book on the market today. Most of them were written by or for fast-track professionals, but they will work for any level of candidate who is willing to use them correctly. These letters are part of a job-search strategy that will allow you to overcome powerful competition and win interviews and job offers.

If you want to learn how to write the kind of letter that can make a busy employer accept your telephone call, this book is for you. If you want to learn how to write a letter that will make an executive secretary march into his boss's office and say, "I think you'd better take a look at this," this book is for you. If you want to learn to write letters that will crack the hidden job market, this book is definitely for you.

You will learn how to design a letter that makes your presentation stand out in a stack of hundreds or even thousands. More importantly, you will learn proven methods to avoid landing in that stack in the first place.

This thin volume covers the whole range of letters you will need in your job search, not just letters for responding to newspaper ads and headhunters' calls, but also:

- Letters to friends and networking contacts
- Broadcast letters to get past gatekeepers and reach decision-makers inside companies
- Thank-you letters to impress employers *after* your interview
- Continuing interest letters, to remind employers of your candidacy
- Offer-acceptance and offer-rejection letters
- Reference sheets and salary histories

Finally, this book covers letters of recommendation, a topic that few business books mention. If you ask for a letter of recommendation and your boss says, "You draft it and I'll sign it," you have the opportunity of a lifetime. The chapter on letters of recommendation tells you how to make yourself sound like your company's most important and valued employee.

This book is designed to be used as a stand-alone guide to writing cover letters, or as a companion to my two other professional-level job-search guides, *The Overnight Résumé* and *The Overnight Job Change Strategy*. If you need either or both of these books, see your local bookseller or call Ten Speed Press at 800-841-BOOK or 510-845-8414, or call my office at 415-543-2020. You can have them delivered in under 48 hours.

Remember to Put Yourself into Your Letters

As you craft your job-change letters, remember that there are no hard-and-fast rules for job-hunting. Some job-search specialists would have you believe that their way is the only way, or that if you don't follow their advice precisely you will end up unemployed forever, or, if you are employed, that you will never get another promotion as long as you live. That is bunk. In my *Overnight* books I've tried to present a job-search method that is systematic, comprehensive, and unbeatable for generating job offers quickly, but my system is hardly the only way to look for work.

One of the unusual things about the job market is the incredibly wide range of techniques that can bring success. You can forget about job letters entirely, hang a sign around your neck, and hand out résumés downtown at lunchtime, and eventually you'll probably get a job. You can go against all current job-search wisdom and conduct your job search strictly through the newspaper want-ads, and eventually you will probably get a position of some kind. In fact, you could send a reasonably coherent cover letter to everyone listed in the Minneapolis telephone directory, and I'll bet you'd get several interviews.

Although the letters in this book are proven performers, be comfortable in deviating from them to suit your own job search, local market conditions, and personality. Let your letters evolve. They will in all probability get better and better as your job search progresses, and be more and more representative of your personality and the job skills you have to offer your next employer.

Chapter One
How People Get Jobs

The Hidden Job Market

Depending on which reports you read, between 70 and 85 percent of all people working today got their current job without reading a newspaper ad or being contacted by a headhunter. They heard about the job from a friend, family member, or more distant acquaintance, or they contacted the company on their own and just happened to be in the right place at the right time.

In short, **they got that job by talking to somebody**. This is what is meant by the *hidden job market*.

The "open" job market, on the other hand, consists of announced openings. Announced openings are advertised in newspaper help-wanted sections, listed with employment agencies and headhunters, entered into on-line computer services provided by every state's employment development department, or posted on bulletin boards or signs in shop windows. The overwhelming majority of jobs are never announced at all, however, and

they will certainly be *hidden* from someone whose search is limited to reading the newspaper and visiting employment agencies.

Most employers know they need help weeks if not months before they place an ad in the newspaper or an order with a placement specialist. During the time between when an employer realizes that she needs help and when the job opening is announced, she is highly susceptible to a query from an interested and qualified jobseeker. A formal placement search takes time and money, and most managers would skip the whole task if a viable candidate appeared at the right time.

The employer saves time and money by selecting a viable candidate before an elaborate placement process is put in motion. The advantage to the candidate is even more substantial: the candidate doesn't have to compete with dozens, if not hundreds, of other candidates.

In a highly competitive selection process, employers can be ridiculously picky. If they want a left-handed, redheaded candidate from Alabama with ten years of experience who is willing to work for 20 percent less than the industry standard, they can find one.

So the smart money is on the hidden job market. That doesn't mean you shouldn't read the help-wanted ads or take that phone call from a headhunter—you should most certainly do both of these things—but it *does* mean that you should base the overwhelming majority of your job-search effort on the hidden job market.

The Best Advertising in the World Is Word of Mouth

A savvy candidate will maximize the number of people he talks to about his job search. Word-of-mouth advertising works both ways: companies get word of your candidacy, and you get word of potential employers. Here are some people that you should talk to as early in your job search as possible:

- Family members
- Friends
- Acquaintances
- Employers, former employers, coworkers, former coworkers
- Clients and customers of current or former employers
- Vendors, suppliers, and business partners
- Classmates, professors, and teachers
- Club and association members
- Members of your church, temple, mosque, or ashram
- Neighbors and former neighbors

Of course if you don't want your current employer to know you are on the job market, you will need to exercise some discretion, but as a rule of thumb, the more people you talk to about your job search, the more people will be able to help you with ideas, leads, referrals, and maybe even outright job offers. You will learn how to approach these contacts properly in chapter 4, "Networking Letters."

Next, you want to talk to potential employers! You cannot run an effective job search without calling up employers and *talking* to them. No matter how good your background, no matter how compelling your letters and résumés, you cannot run an aggressive campaign by just licking stamps. You absolutely must get in the habit of calling potential employers whenever you write to them. This is covered more fully in chapter 5, "Broadcast Letters for Targeted Companies."

To build a lead list of employers to contact, try some of these resources:

- The business yellow pages for your targeted area
- Industry directories and other resource guides published for your industry

- Trade association membership lists, available from the association headquarters
- The reference desk of your community's public library
- Chambers of commerce lists
- Geographically based job guides listing all employers in a specific area
- General job guides listing major firms nationwide
- The *articles* in the business section of your local or regional newspaper
- The *articles* in the trade press for your profession
- The *articles* in the national business press (*Wall Street Journal, Fortune, Barrons,* etc.)
- The classified help-wanted section of local, regional, or national newspapers
- Database companies such as Dun & Bradstreet that sell data on millions of companies

Be sure to check in with your local library and bookseller *at least.*

Telephone Protocol

When you call networking contacts and potential employers, as you will be instructed to do repeatedly in this book, you need to have a sophisticated business telephone manner. First of all, **respect those secretaries and receptionists.** There is no more sure way to torpedo your chances with an employer than to alienate the people who control the flow of information and appointments within that organization. Be nice, be friendly, and remember *they* have a job to do too. That said, however, here are some tips to get you past the gatekeepers to the decision-makers:

- Quit fooling around and just pick up the phone and call, once a day, for a minimum of seven business days, until you get through (leave a polite message each time if you don't reach your intended party).
- Call early, call late, and call during lunchtime, when the gatekeeper is not on duty.
- Mention in your cover letter exactly when you will be calling, so you can say, "Yes, she's expecting my call."
- Cite a referral source.
- If you get voicemail, make an appointment for your next call, such as, "I'll try again tomorrow at exactly 10:00 A.M." The next day at 10:00, if you get voicemail again, have them paged.
- Dial around the front desk until you reach someone who is not a gatekeeper. For example, if the main number is 555-6500, try 555-6501, 555-6502, 555-6503, until you reach somebody friendly.

Be careful not to call the same person more than once a day, and remember to be polite, but other than that, it's probably better to err on the side of persistence. Persistence and diligence are virtues in an employee, and you can demonstrate them before you ever even talk to your targeted decision-maker.

Be Comprehensive and Systematic

You crack the hidden job market by talking to people, and you will find it much easier to talk to people if you write to them first, using the techniques in this book. You may have picked up this book because you need to write a letter by tomorrow morning in response to a newspaper ad or a call from a headhunter, but I sincerely hope you will go on to adopt a comprehensive and systematic approach to your job search. Target *every* employer with the potential to hire you, write to *every* target, and call *every* time you write.

Also, unless you are currently employed, you need to work forty hours per week on your job search. The best pattern is to work Sunday afternoon through Friday afternoon. Use Sunday to plan your coming week and write letters to some of the ads in the Sunday paper. Knock off all job-search efforts on Friday afternoon. Even if you manage to reach decision-makers then, they will be shutting down their week, not planning new and greater things like being smart enough to hire you. Forty hours per week! Make yourself a job-search time card and punch in and out like a factory worker. Prove to yourself that you are really putting in the time and effort it takes to land that next job.

If you are currently employed, looking for work can be your night job. Use every lunchtime and break to make those phone calls. Even if you work nine hours a day, five days a week, you still have 123 hours left each and every week to look for work.

For more on job-search strategies, identifying potential target companies and decision-makers, creating a network from scratch, getting past gatekeepers, and every other phase of the search from plotting a career path to interviewing, see my book, *The Overnight Job Change Strategy.*

Chapter Two
Components of Compelling Job-Search Letters

Who Is This Letter For?

Before you finish this chapter you will have written at least one good job-search letter. If you do not actually need a letter right away, choose a hypothetical employer and draft a prototype. Take out a piece of paper right now and write down the targeted recipient of your letter. (If you have trouble getting started, try defining your targeted recipient by title and industry, as in "vice president of sales for a software company.")

If you have a specific target, write down what you know about them, "Mr. Jamie Johnson, my cousin Bob's boss, engineer, runs quality assurance for Dynamo Magnetics, always wears a suit even to company picnics, plays bridge."

You may have a newspaper ad that specifies your target, "recruiter, ad #2185, c/o Metro Newspapers," or perhaps something more personal, "résumé and letter to Barbra, Human Resources, Dylsexics Untie, Inc."

Write down your target now. Pick only one, and start the whole process over again for subsequent letters. **Don't read further until you have pulled out some paper and written down your target!**

Remember, your letter is going to land on a real person's desk. Before you begin to write, sit down and think about your intended recipient for a moment. In fact, close your eyes right now and imagine somebody receiving the letter you are about to write.

See her picking up that stack of incoming mail? See her rip open several letters before yours? See her cut into your envelope flap with a letter opener? Can you feel the paper, see her read, anticipate her thoughts? What's on her mind? She has exactly two questions: "What the heck do I do with this letter?" and "What can this candidate do for me (or my boss)?"

Those are pretty important questions, and you'd better answer them. In a sense, the whole rest of this book is about how to answer these two questions in a compelling manner. As you draft your job-search letters, think of what will interest this reader. Remember that she will be more interested in what you can do for her than what she can do for you.

Be confident and forthcoming, but don't sound arrogant. If at all possible, banish the following shopworn terms: "proactive," "self-motivated," "team player," "well organized," and "strong written and oral communication skills." Is there any manager in the history of business who doesn't think he fits such a description? Likewise forgo vague adjectives like "outstanding," "excellent," "impressive," "significant." In the following sections we will get into what you *should* include, but for now let's concentrate on this reader as she glances over your letter. She is likely to be your toughest critic, and you'd better answer those two questions of hers quickly, repeatedly, and well.

- **What the heck do I do with this letter?**
- **What can this candidate do for me or my boss?**

The Heading

Now that you have some paper out and know whom you are writing to, you can build a job-search letter piece by piece. This is just a first draft, so don't worry about how it looks, just do each section as you come to it. You can fix the layout later. If you have several targets picked out, focus on only one until you finish your first letter.

First, you need a heading. If you are enclosing a résumé with your letter, try to make the headings match. You must include *at least* your name, mailing address, and home telephone number. Be sure your home phone line has a functioning message machine with a business-like outgoing message. You cannot conduct an effective job search without a viable twenty-four-hour messaging system.

With the exception of routine government placements, employers are overwhelmingly likely to make their initial contact by telephone. They will probably call only once; if they don't reach you, they will go on to the next candidate. Be sure that your entire name, address, and phone number are part of your heading, and not hidden some-

where in the body of your letter. The classical style for a social letter, with the return address and phone at the bottom, is not advisable in a job-search setting.

Because instantaneous communication has become critical in business life, multiple communication methods are commonly listed in the headings to letters and résumés. You may choose to list a business telephone number, as well as voicemail, fax, pager, car phone, and answering service numbers. However, as long as you have one fail-safe twenty-four-hour message number, and you check it daily, you don't necessarily need to list anything more.

If you are currently living in one area but looking for work in another, it can be very helpful to list addresses for both locales. You can rent a box from a mail-drop service, or use a friend or relative's address. If you are planning to move soon, you may wish to list old and new addresses, noting *Address until August 1* and *Address as of August 1,* for example.

Make it as easy as possible for employers to contact you, and they will be more likely to do so.

❀

Underneath your address, list the date and the addressee, in that order. Keep your dates simple, either "August 8, 1994" or "8 August 1994." All the dates in the heading and the body of your letter should follow the same format. Never send a job-search letter without a date on it. Many companies file letters by date, and the absence will be glaringly noted.

❀

Next, list the addressee by name, title, company name, street address, city, state, and zip code. You can either stack the name and title, or put the title after the name:

Jordan Wallace, V.P., Finance

　　or

Jordan Wallace
V.P., Finance

Do not use a double title (a common error that you should avoid).

Incorrect:	Correct:
Dr. Jayne Louter, Ph.D.	Dr. Jayne Louter
	or
	Jayne Louter, Ph.D.
Ms. J. L. Snippet, V.P., Taxation	J. L. Snippet, V.P., Taxation
Mr. Julian Bond, Esq.	Julian Bond, Esq.
Ms. K. T. Larynx, R.N.	K. T. Larynx, R.N.

Write to a person by name, not to a company. If you simply cannot get an exact name, write to a title, as in "Vice President of Sales."

Whenever possible you should know your addressee's correct, exact name and title. If you do not have this information, or if you are not sure of its accuracy, pick up the phone and call the targeted company. Do not ask to speak with your intended recipient, but do ask to verify spelling and title. If they ask you why, you can simply say, "I am preparing a mailing to Dr. Zerkowskilenski, and I just want to make sure I have her name spelled correctly."

If you don't know your addressee's name, you can often get it by calling and asking for the person by her title: "Hello, I am preparing a mailing to your office manager, and I'm afraid I don't know his or her name. Can you help me with that?" Be sure to follow up with, "How do you spell that?" and "Is her correct title 'Office Manager'?" Misspelling someone's name will usually result in your letter being discarded pronto. You will not always get the name you want when you call and ask, but often you will—certainly a lot more often than if you don't call at all.

As mentioned above, if you cannot get an exact name, address your letter to an approximate title for the department head or other decision-maker you want:

Vice President of Sales

Chief Engineer

M.I.S. Manager

Office Manager

Hiring Partner

In general, write to a line manager, that is, someone who would be your direct supervisor, or *his* direct supervisor. Try to avoid writing to the human resources department unless specifically instructed to do so in a job announcement. Even then, it is a good idea to send a separate letter and résumé to the pertinent line manager. (For more on how to identify specific individuals within a targeted organization, see *The Overnight Job Change Strategy.*)

※

Phrasing the salutation is easy. If you are writing to an individual, it is simply "Dear" followed by the title and last name, as in "Dear Dr. Louter:". If you know the person well, you may choose to address him by his first name, but it is usually not recommended in a business letter. Always use a colon to close your salutation, never a comma. The comma is reserved for intimate social communiqués, and is inappropriate in all business settings.

If you are unable to find out your intended recipient's gender, *do not guess!* Use the person's initials—"Dear J. L. Snippet:"—or title and last name—"Dear Vice President Snippet:". Watch out for unusual or foreign first names, and names like Chris and Kelly, which could belong to either a male or a female. If you get someone's gender wrong, you can forget about your message's impact. The only impact it will make will be in the round file where it will land at high speed.

Unless you are writing to the All Strictly and Only Men's Club, never write to "Dear Sir:" or "Dear Sirs:". This antiquarian style of address will not win you any friends in the contemporary business world, even if your recipient accidentally happens to be male. Do not use the titles "Miss" or "Mrs." in a business setting, regardless of the recipient's age or marital status.

If you do not have a name to write to, you can use the same business or professional title in the salutation as you used in the address.

Dear Vice President of Sales:

Dear Quality Assurance Manager:

Dear Placement Specialist:

Dear Counselor:

If you are writing to a group, address them collectively. The plural of "Dr." is "Drs." The plural of "Mr." is "Messrs." The plural of "Ms." is "Mss." Here are some examples:

Dear Members of the Search Committee:

Ladies and Gentlemen:

Dear Drs. Johansson and Johansson:

Dear Mss. Boatwright and Sieworthy:

When all else fails, address the letter "Dear Prospective Employer:".

Whether you are writing a first draft by hand or have a computer humming away, waiting to receive your masterpiece, *draft your heading now.* Again, don't worry about spacing; you can fix that later. The main thing is to get your first draft down and go on. Do not get stuck playing around with your heading: we have much more important tasks coming right up.

Examples of letter headings:

B. JOHN "JACK" WALLACE

c/o Mailtron Forwarding, Inc.
Box 1640
1200 Broadway
New York, New York 10010
U.S.A.
Message: (217) 555-7611, Ridgefield, Illinois, U.S.A.

#1480 Asahi Ambision Ebisu
1-57-32 Ebisu Minami
Shibuya-Ku
Tokyo 145
JAPAN
Office/Voicemail: (81-3) 3245-3482
Residence/Fax/Message: (81-3) 3275-8203

May 1, 1995

Alferd Packer
General Manager
Wild West Expeditions
1000 Eldorado Fields Drive
Boulder, Colorado 80303
(303) 555-1842

Dear Mr. Packer:

(body of letter starts here)

Robert Zimmerman
1304 Midwood Place
Silver Spring, Maryland 20910
Office: (301) 555-1252
Residence: (301) 555-1257

February 2, 1995

William Harrison, Chief Financial Officer
Watkins Realty & Auctions, Inc.
11901 Maumelle Boulevard
Maumelle, Arkansas 72113

Dear Mr. Harrison:

(body of letter starts here)

The Opening

Since most recipients will not read your heading at all, the first few lines in the body are the most critical in the entire letter. If you want someone to care about what you're saying, you have to get her attention right away. Most job-search letters start out with a very predictable first paragraph, something like this:

> In the interest of discussing employment opportunities with your organization, I have enclosed my résumé for your review.

This is a perfectly functional opening, but it lacks pizzazz. It is not compelling. It won't win any prizes for sex appeal. In fact, it's boring.

More promising openings are what I call the **you asked for it,** the **personal referral,** the **hook line,** the **news commentary**, and the **let me keep this exceedingly brief**.

In the **you asked for it** opening, you remind your reader from the very first line that this letter was solicited. If you spoke with the recipient and she was anything less than rude to you, remind her of how she encouraged you to send the enclosed information. Here is an example:

> As you requested in our telephone conversation on Monday, I am forwarding my résumé for your review. I certainly appreciate your enthusiasm for my candidacy! As a former officer of First Interstellar, with experience in mortgage loan origination and processing and a business systems specialist with an extensive background—most of it directly related to your needs—you can imagine how excited *I* was to read your advertisement . . .

Whew! Better call this person right away and hire her before she gets away. Here are two milder versions of the **you asked for it** opening:

> I was very encouraged by your interest in my candidacy. I've enclosed my résumé for further consideration.

✿

> As was requested by your office, I have enclosed my résumé for your consideration.

In a literal sense, you could use that last intro in response to any announced opening, whether you have spoken with anyone or not, as long as the advertisement said something like, "Send résumé and cover letter to . . ."

If you were referred to the company by anyone, be sure to mention your **personal referral** in the first sentence. Here are some examples:

> Maryjo Bowie, the manufacturing planner at your Winston site, alerted me to your need for a mechanical engineer with a strong background in TQM and statistical analysis. At her suggestion, I am writing to you directly.

> ❁

> Your neighbor, Lynda Highbred, had awfully nice things to say about you at a dinner last night, and she suggested that you might be able to help me with my job search. My expertise is . . .

> ❁

> Your accounting manager, Marjorie Lewis, has been encouraging me to meet with you. She thinks I have something unique to offer Decker Communications and its clients, especially in the area of customer service training for blue- and pink-collar workers. Currently I am a stand-up comedian . . .

> ❁

> I was discussing remote sensing technologies with Jerome Levinson of M.I.T., and he suggested that you might be interested in someone with my background. I've enclosed my résumé for your review.

You should list a referral whenever you can, as this is one of the best ways to get past those secretaries and clerks who are instructed to screen unsolicited applications. Even if your targeted recipient doesn't know Jerome Levinson from Adam, the clerk will have to forward your letter to be sure. You want your letter read by a decision-maker, not routed by clerks to clerks who generate a nice little form letter that reads something like this: "Thank you for your recent application for employment. While we were impressed by your qualifications . . ."

If you cannot find a mutual acquaintance of any kind, here is a special kind of personal referral that has proved highly effective for some of my clients:

> I was very interested to read in the *Los Angeles Times* about your efforts to assist the Russians in rebuilding their agricultural infrastructure. I've asked around to see if we have any mutual acquaintances, and the closest I've been able to come is that my business partner, Barton Taylor, was your brother Simon's advisor at the University of Texas many, many years ago. I had wanted a more personal introduction, but I hope you won't mind if I just write to you directly.

You can even boil this intro down to, "Since we don't seem to have any mutual acquaintances, I hope you won't mind if I take the liberty of writing to you directly." It might come off as a little blunt, so be prepared to follow with a compelling letter.

The **hook line** is a technique borrowed from direct-mail advertising. When sending an unsolicited mailing to a total stranger, you have about one sentence to entice your recipient to read further. In the hook line opening, you do this by introducing a thought they'll find intriguing or important. For example:

> Do you want a sales professional who can convert a wrong number into an appointment? I recently did just that, and the result was a sale! Just imagine what I can do for you when I'm working with qualified leads.

> ❁

> Don't you just love it when it's done right the first time? If you're going to go through the time and trouble to develop new systems and applications, why not have them specified and developed right the first time. That makes sense to me, too.

> ❁

> Will your five-year plan for administrative operations facilitate your strategic business plans, or are the administrative systems in your firm reactive, tardy, always two steps behind your strategic plans?

The following hook line was used with great success by a recent college graduate:

If energy, youth, and vitality were all I had to offer you, I probably wouldn't even bother writing this letter.

Hook lines are not always substantive. Some of them are just odd. My all-time favorite is, "People told me I was crazy when . . ." For the letter that uses that line, and more examples of good hook lines, see chapter 5, "Broadcast Letters for Targeted Companies."

The **news commentary** opening demonstrates that you are a savvy candidate who has already researched the company in question. One example is listed above, in which the writer cites an article he saw in the *Los Angeles Times*. Here are a few more:

> When I read the article about your development group ("Software publisher solves holographic imaging problem," *Future NOW!,* June 1994), I was just about ready to pack my bags and move to Boston. This is the same software problem I worked on at Games to Fame here in San Jose.

✿

> I was very interested to read of your new rasterizing process in a recent *Wall Street Journal* article. I immediately thought of a potential new application which may be of interest to you.

✿

> I read with great interest of your plans to expand into Latin American markets (*Des Moines Register,* 8/12/94). As an export manager with 8 years of experience selling to Latin American markets, I think we may have something to discuss.

The **let me keep this exceedingly brief** intro is exactly that, a promise that reading your letter and considering your proposal will only take a few more seconds. Do *not* use this opening unless the letter that follows is brief, concise, and to the point. Here are two versions:

> For your convenience, I will keep this exceedingly brief. I am interested in obtaining a position with your company. My background would make me most appropriate for . . .

✿

> I am interested in having a short face-to-face talk with you about opportunities in commercial real estate.

Draft your introduction now. Use one of the introductions listed here:

you asked for it

personal referral

hook line

news commentary

let me keep this exceedingly brief

The first, reminding them that they asked you to apply, is probably the strongest opening, followed by the personal referral. The hook line, news commentary, and let me keep this exceedingly brief openings are probably about equally effective, so choose the one that most appeals to you.

Remember, this is just a first draft. If you have trouble crafting your introduction, you can fall back on a version of one of the following two examples. They are not too sexy, but they will never be inappropriate.

> In the interest of obtaining a position with your company, I have enclosed a copy of my résumé for your review.

✿

> Please accept this letter and the enclosed résumé in application for the position of Benefits Analyst II.

The Rationale

The rationale portion of your cover letter conveys what you want the employer to know about your experience and abilities. This can be the heart of a cover letter but, ironically, it is entirely optional. When you combine your letter with a highly targeted résumé, your career information is readily available on the very next page, and your letter can be more of a routing slip. In this case, it serves to make sure your résumé gets to the right person, tells them what type of position you are interested in, and directs their attention to your résumé.

For your first draft, go ahead and develop a rationale. You can decide later whether to keep it. Even if you do decide later to omit this section, writing it is great preparation for an interview.

In effect, this middle portion of your letter provides the reason, the *rationale,* for why your intended recipient should want to speak with you. This is especially important when writing to strangers, when you are an unusual candidate, and when your résumé does not support your candidacy as strongly as you would like.

Before writing your rationale section, complete the following two exercises:

Exercise #1:
Make a list of ten to thirty accomplishments that you consider the greatest of your life. If this is the first time you have ever made such a list, take your time. Be sure to consider your entire life, including work, education, and social life, and volunteer, family, and leisure-time experiences.

Exercise #2:
Step 1: Write down the exact title of the position you would like to hold.

Step 2: List the **skills, talents, knowledge, aptitudes,** and **experience** that an *ideal candidate* for this title would have.

Step 3: Considering your entire work, educational, social, volunteer, family, and leisure experiences, provide concrete evidence that you possess the skills, talents, knowledge, aptitudes, and background that an ideal candidate would have.

In other words, prepare a list of past accomplishments and past experiences that demonstrate your ability to perform in the targeted position.

These are standard job-search exercises. You may have done similar exercises when preparing your résumé. Do not proceed one step further with your job search until you have completed these two basic exercises.

✺

A rationale section is particularly useful for presenting information that would be inappropriate to include in a traditional business résumé. For example, your parents' occupations, your life before you began college, and your hobbies have no place in most modern résumés, but could easily be woven into a persuasive rationale section:

> I have enclosed a copy of my master's thesis on the African influences in American Christian religious symbolism, which I researched during my internship with the Smithsonian. In addition to my undergraduate education in Spanish and Latin languages, you may find it particularly pertinent that I lived in Brazil from the ages of 4 to 15, and am completely fluent in Portuguese (speak/read/write/translate). My mother was a professor of history and an amateur hagiographer, and my father was plant manager for a company that manufactured religious statuary for churches all over the world. Finally, I have collected religious artifacts privately for over a decade. I think this background makes me uniquely qualified for the position of acquisitions curator as you build your collection of New World iconography.

Your experiences may not be this exotic, but this is an illustration of how one can use the letter to convey critical information that does not belong on a résumé. Of course, include only material that is relevant to the type of position you are seeking.

The rationale section can also be used to discuss such issues as:

Why you are leaving. Put this information in a positive light, or don't mention it at all. Headhunters are more interested in this issue than most employers, but mentioning it is purely optional in either case. Here are two sample paragraphs:

> My current employer is very happy with my performance, but due to market pressures, little growth opportunity is on the horizon at a time when I wish to expand my responsibilities. If you can introduce me to companies where I can contribute to my fullest ability, I would be most responsive to your assistance.

❂

> I take great pride in my work, and I have an excellent reputation with all my former employers. Although my current employer is quite happy with my performance, the firm is undergoing some organizational challenges that have led me to consider looking outside. If you can offer a challenging position with a talented team, then I can offer you competence, the desire to perform, and availability for overtime and special projects as needed.

Your salary history or requirements. As a general rule, you shouldn't mention anything about salary history or requirements. These are always exclusionary data (that is, information used only to disqualify you). If you are writing to a headhunter or responding to an advertisement that requests such data, see chapter 6, "Broadcast Letters for Headhunters," or chapter 3, "Cover Letters for Announced Openings," for further guidance.

Why you are relocating. Be sure to state that you *are* relocating, not that you are *considering* relocating. If you can gently malign the region you are leaving while praising the region you are moving to, all the better.

Here is an example:

> Upon my graduation from the UCLA tax program, my wife and I will not be staying in California. We have started a family (baby girl, Courtney, one year old). As you might imagine, California is no place to raise a child. What with earthquakes, crime, increasingly dangerous socio-economic tensions, and astronomical housing costs, we are looking forward to returning to the gentility of the Southeast. My wife and I are both from Georgia, and we have family there, so the transition will be an easy one.

Here is an opposing view:

> My husband and I are looking forward to our return to Southern California. Although we have enjoyed aspects of our time here, we are both eager to return to civilization.

Unless you are at the executive level, be sure to indicate that you will pay your own way to an interview, or you will lose the offer to readily available local talent. Alternately, you can set up interview junkets—let employers know that you will be in town only briefly, and that they should take advantage of this opportunity to meet with you.

For example:

> I will be relocating to Minneapolis in May. Early next month I will be in the Twin Cities for ten days, and would like to meet with you or your designated representative at that time to explore potential for mutual interest.

Why the employer should consider an unusual candidate. This is one of the trickiest rationales that a letter-writer will ever present. First, consider how to turn a liability into an asset. Next, try to emphasize a corresponding weakness that the leading candidates are likely to have.

For example:

> Although you may be inundated with the résumés of training specialists from related fields, such as the cosmetics and retail industries, I feel that I have a great deal more to offer precisely because of the breadth of my background.

❖

> This job is exactly one step up for me, which means that I will be excited by it and more than happy to give it 110%, whereas someone with much more experience than myself might take a blasé approach.

❖

> Although you may not have anticipated an application from someone such as myself, I think you can see that I have the potential to really excel in this position. You want results, and that's what I can deliver. I believe my age will be a tremendous asset in dealing with your client base, and once we meet in a personal interview, I think you will agree.

❖

> You should select me because I don't have any experience. I will learn to do it your way and I'll be responsive to your training and guidance. Why should you spend your time battling someone else's bad habits, when you can just show me how to do it right in the first place?

Mention reasons for relocation or leaving your job, or unusual aspects of your candidacy *only* when you feel something would be an issue for the reader. In the majority of letters, the rationale section should focus on skills and experience.

Highlight your accomplishments with action language like the following—some of my favorite action verbs:

advised	established	negotiated	reorganized
analyzed	guided	orchestrated	resolved
conducted	hired	organized	revised
created	increased	originated	started
designed	initiated	overhauled	streamlined
developed	managed	oversaw	supervised
devised	maximized	planned	tested
directed	motivated	promoted	trained

Use superlatives whenever you can to report your accomplishments, particularly:

most	highest
best	largest
all	top
only	first

Accomplishments can be listed a thousand different ways. The following formulas describe three popular, effective ways to present them:

STAR (**S**ituation, **T**ask, **A**ction, **R**esult). For example:

> I was temporarily assigned to take over the accounting department after the manager had a heart attack. My task was to regain cohesion in the group and keep our workflow on schedule. Since I was supervising people who used to be peers and would be again, it was a sensitive assignment. I met privately with every single member of staff, asking for their faith and cooperation and offering mine in return. We pulled together and got the budget in on time. I know I have the kind of supervisory skills you need if you've just had a reorganization.

PSR (**P**roblem, **S**olution, **R**esult). For example:

> The aperture was jamming 42% of the time on oblique load, so I recommended turning it down for gravity assist. With the new protocol, we had a 82% reduction in jamming and got client sign-off for a critical work-in-progress disbursement. If this is the type of common-sense engineering you want on your team, let's talk further.

PAR (**P**roblem, **A**ction, **R**esult). For example:

> In my last job I noticed that all the staff looked pretty droopy by late afternoon, so I started serving afternoon tea in the executive suite. It may seem like a small thing, but it really helped boost morale and productivity.

Of course, you can skip the details and just list the result: "Increased Widget sales by 17%." At the risk of insulting your intelligence, the best rule of thumb is "keep it short and make it sound good."

Draft your rationale now. Be sure to answer the primary question in your reader's mind: **What can this candidate do for me or my boss?**

Here are some more examples:

> My entire background has been in the travel business, working with both business and leisure travel markets. My skills encompass marketing and strategic sales planning, key account development, training/coaching of sales professionals, development of marketing materials, and selection/implementation of PC systems for account administration, lead management, and client databasing.

With my uncommon combination of experience, I was surprised to find a job announcement that seemed written for me. Pertinent to your requirements, I have the following:

- Over five years of experience in local government planning in Arizona, including departmental budgeting.

- Master of City Planning degree with emphasis on real-estate development issues, and including finance studies in the graduate school of business.

- Hands-on experience in planning and management for a major Arizona-Nevada developer, including comprehensive project financial analysis.

- Directly applicable consulting experience with local governments, on public finance and redevelopment, including report writing and final presentations to the client.

- Full responsibility for developing required analytical methodologies.

❖

Perhaps you will be interested in the following accomplishments:

- Coplanned worldwide market expansion efforts, identifying most promising countries and market segments within those countries, and developing successful strategies to crack those markets.

- Increased European sales by more than 100% over prior year. Expanded the dealer/distributor network *and* increased direct sales efforts.

- Demonstrated rapid learning curve with new products and markets.

- Served as bilingual manager, Japanese-English, including knowledge of honorifics and Japanese business protocol. Talent for multicultural sales in general.

I am looking for a product or company that will be a market leader. If you could use someone with my unique background and talents, I am eager for a new challenge.

❖

My background includes extensive experience in aviation-related litigation management, including litigation related to aviation accidents and product liability litigation related to aircraft components and systems. In addition to legal expertise, I think I could bring unique skills to a position with your firm: graduate-level technical education in both aeronautical engineering and aviation accident investigation, a capacity for science and technology issues, extensive experience as a test pilot and a manager of aviation research projects, and an effective combination of expertise and energy.

Other areas of experience include independent department management, selection and management of consultants, selection and management of outside counsel, trends analysis, and provision of advice and counsel to senior policy- and decision-makers.

Even a recent college graduate with little relevant background can write an enthusiastic rationale for why she would make a good employee:

As you can see from the attached, I am a recent college graduate with a strong liberal arts education. My greatest strength would have to be my communication skills. I am someone who is able to make things happen. I applied for and thoroughly enjoyed a year abroad, held several elected offices in school, and started a local chapter of a national sorority. I have all the routine office skills, as well as organizational abilities demonstrated in several internships listed on my résumé.

Do not read further until you have drafted at least one version of a rationale for why an employer should believe you could perform on their behalf.

The Call to Action!

So far your letter has gotten your reader's attention, given him a reason to read it, and convinced him that you have something to offer. Now what? The call to action, perhaps the most critical component of any job-search letter. **What do you want to happen next?**

What action do you, as a candidate, want out of the employer? Ironically, you do *not* want a (premature) job offer. Employers are not impressed by letters that ask for jobs. After all, do you really know you would want a job with that company? How could they know they want to hire you just from your letter and résumé? Do you really want a job before you know exactly what it requires or find out more about the company and the people you'll be working with?

You should be seeking a good fit, and that is a two-way street. Signal this with language like: "discuss this further," "explore the potential for mutual interest," "conversation," and "discussion." Incidentally, when you can, try to avoid asking for an interview. Employers dislike interviews, but everybody in the world enjoys a good conversation or discussion. If you use the word "meeting," put "brief" in front of it.

Your immediate goal, then, is a telephone conversation, and, when you reach the person who can hire you for the type of position you want, a face-to-face interview *whether they are hiring or not*. You cannot be hired over the phone, you cannot make a lasting impression over the phone, you cannot evaluate a company or an opportunity over the phone, so you want an interview. You want an interview whether or not they are hiring because that's how the hidden job market works. They may not be hiring now, but when that next opportunity comes up, if they already know you and what you have to offer, they won't need to search—they can just call you. Of course, you will need to contact them periodically for the duration of your job search to remind them of your availability.

When dealing with a networking lead, or anyone but a hiring authority, ask for ideas, leads, and referrals by telephone. You can fill up your calendar with inefficient meetings with friends and acquaintances when you could get all the information you need by telephone. Besides, you'll be spending a lot of money on restaurant and bar tabs, money that you may need if your job search takes longer than expected.

In short, here's the action plan for your job-search mailings:

IF CONTACT IS:	A hiring authority for the type of position you want	Anyone else
STEP ONE:	Send a letter.	Send a letter.
STEP TWO:	Have a telephone conversation.	Have a telephone conversation.
STEP THREE:	Get appointment for face-to-face meeting.	Get ideas, leads, referrals.

In every case, your immediate goal is a telephone conversation. Your **call to action** should do exactly what it says, spur the employer to action either to pick up the phone and call you or to accept your telephone call. Most job-search letters are woefully inadequate in this regard. Even some of the most qualified candidates have weak calls to action, like:

Please contact me if you are interested in exploring this further.

What disdain! What total lack of zeal! The employer certainly knows what to do with this letter: throw it away without further delay.

Unless an employer just happens to be desperate to hire someone with the letter writer's exact qualifications, a passive close is a grave error. It leaves the ball in the employer's court; the candidate loses both control and momentum.

Here is a much better call to action:

On this Thursday before noon I will call your office to see what suggestions and ideas you may have for me. Please advise your secretary to expect my call.

A good call to action will answer the question, **What the heck do I do with this letter?** The answer is, hang on to it until this woman calls on Thursday.

Making an exact appointment for a telephone call can be impressive, "I will call precisely at 10:00 A.M. on Thursday," but don't be overly precise if you cannot follow through. If you say you will call on Thursday at 10:00 A.M., that means you must call between 9:58:00 and 9:59:59. From 10:00:00 to 10:00:59 you are late, and after 10:01:00 your credibility evaporates rapidly. Be careful to make only those promises that you can keep.

As mentioned earlier, an added benefit of specifying that you will call is that you can answer, "Is she expecting your call?" with a simple "Yes." You can *always* answer, "And may I tell him what this is regarding?" with "I mailed him some materials last week. He will be expecting my call."

Schedule your follow-up call very close to the letter's arrival. Nobody is going to hang on to a letter just because you said you'd call "within ten days." You must call within forty-eight hours of your letter's arrival, or you will have lost all momentum, and they will have lost your letter.

This means that you need to be able to estimate when the letter will arrive. Figure one to two business days locally; for longer distances, it's worth it to spend the extra money for two-day priority mail, or even overnight delivery.

It can be a good idea to use your call to action to remind the employer that you are not necessarily going to ask them for a job, that, after an exploratory conversation, you may ask for ideas, leads, and referrals instead. Here is one way to do this:

> At this time I am not applying for a particular position. I am just interested in having a brief "get acquainted" meeting to see if we can establish a mutual interest, and to see how my background might be of use to you. Would you have a moment to get together for such a meeting? Even if you don't anticipate any openings, I'd still like to meet briefly to see what ideas you may have for me. I will call you within 48 hours of your receipt of this letter.

Of course, all these techniques are based on the assumption that you are writing to a specific person by name, and that you are the sort of person who can make a cold call and introduce yourself. It may help to script these calls in advance, preparing something like this: "Hello, Ms. Hardwon? This is Clyde Antony. I'm the one who sent you the letter inquiring about possible positions in accounting. I believe you got that letter yesterday. If you will remember, I have three years of experience in . . ."

If for any reason you cannot discover the exact person to contact at a company you've targeted, you will have to fall back on "Please contact me if you are interested in exploring this further."

Finally, be aware that you will not always meet with or even talk to your targeted recipient. If this seems likely, use your call to action to tell the recipient what she should do with your mailing, for example:

> Since there are many ways in which I could serve the Republican party, I think it would be best if you would assign somebody to speak with me personally. Also, if you think there is some way I can serve the Quayle presidential campaign, please feel free to forward my information to someone who could use it. I am available to my candidate and my party.

In this way you can advise your recipient as to the person or types of person that you want your application forwarded to inside or outside of his organization.

Draft your call to action now. Here are several more examples for guidance:

> I will call you at your office at 10:30 A.M. on Monday to see if we can establish a mutual interest. You can count on me to be punctual. If for any reason you will not be available at that time, please leave word with your secretary as to when would be a more convenient time to call.

✿

Even if you don't anticipate any openings, a moment of your time would be greatly appreciated. I'd like to hear what ideas you may have for me.

Thank you for your consideration. I'll be calling you shortly to see if we can arrange a time to get together.

✿

I hope my background will warrant an interview to discuss this further. My office is not far from yours, and I would be happy to meet with you at your convenience to see if we can establish a mutual interest. Please call me at my home telephone number. If I do not hear from you by next Thursday, I will try to ring your office and check on the status of my application.

✿

I will be calling your office early next week, so please keep this application handy. I am eager to learn more about your requirements. Should we establish a mutual interest by telephone, I would be happy to travel at my own expense to a personal interview.

Thank you for your consideration. I look forward to our conversation.

✿

If you think there is a chance that you will have staff adjustments in my areas of expertise, please consider what I have to offer. Since I am not in a hurry to change jobs, a brief conversation now might save you from conducting an expensive and time-consuming search later on. I'll call your office early next week to discuss this with you personally. If we discover a mutual interest, I can wait until you need me.

If you must use a passive call to action, make it compelling and enthusiastic:

With my experience and background, I am confident that I can make a meaningful and lasting contribution to your (program, organization, firm, company). I would like to meet with you to discuss this further. Please call me at your earliest convenience to arrange a time. I may be reached at (telephone number).

Do not read further until you have drafted at least one call to action for your job-search letter.

The Closing

The final piece consists of your complimentary closing, your name, postscript information, and secretarial notations.

The first word of your complimentary closing should be capitalized; subsequent words should not. The most common complimentary closing is "Sincerely," but you might like to try:

Sincerely yours,

Yours sincerely,

Most sincerely,

Respectfully,

Respectfully yours,

Cordially,

In casual settings, some writers use the last line of the letter as a complimentary closing:

Thank you for your consideration,

The complimentary closing is always followed by a comma, several lines of space, and then your name. Sign your letters between the complimentary closing and your typewritten name, which should appear exactly as it does in the letter's heading. If you normally sign your name "Bill M. Later," it is fine to do so even if your typewritten name reads "William M. Later."

Underneath your name, there should be room for postscript information and secretarial notations. Avoid chatty postscripts; the following are fairly common on job-search letters:

Salary: Negotiable
Enclosure: Résumé
Enclosures
Availability: May 1st, 1994
References to follow by separate cover.
Sent via fax; hard copy to follow.
cc: Jean R. Sullivan, Director of Human Resources
JFK/ml

Use "Salary: Negotiable" to acknowledge that you saw a request for salary data (history or requirements), but chose not to provide the data at this stage of the placement process (see chapter 9, "Salary Histories").

Secretarial notations indicate someone else types your letters. The capitalized letters refer to the author and signatory; the lowercase to the secretary or typist who produced the document: a notation reading "RFA/rm," for example, means that **R**uby **F**aye **A**usbrooks wrote the letter, and **R**obert **M**urdock typed it. Some people have been known to use this convention to invent secretaries they don't have. Secretarial designation is optional in any case.

Draft your closing now. Here are two examples of closings, complete with signatures:

Yours sincerely,

Monique Ross

Monique M. Ross
Enclosure
MMR/dy

✿

Respectfully,

Robert Paul Moorpark

Robert Paul Moorpark
Salary: Negotiable

Congratulations! You have drafted a compelling job-search letter, better than the overwhelming majority of letters most employers will ever see. Sit back, relax, and read it through. Looks pretty good, doesn't it? By concentrating on the parts, you have made a whole with a minimum of effort. Look over your letter noting each component:

Heading

Intro

Rationale

Call to Action

Closing

Now it's time for a quick edit. You're almost ready to get this thing in the mail.

Editing, Design, and Production

The facts are clear: Your letter and résumé will be scanned for just a few seconds. You want those first few seconds to really count. Read through your letter, imagining your intended recipient, or her secretary, opening up the envelope and glancing at what you've just written. What are they going to see? A well-prepared letter filled with compelling information? Or just another piece of junk mail?

This glance test is terribly important. Do you grab your reader's interest right from the very first sentence? Beware of using the first few lines to get warmed up—too many documents begin with what amounts to a verbal clearing of the throat, for example: "Please allow me to introduce myself and why I am writing to you . . ." Would your letter be even stronger if you scratched out the first paragraph or two and started in the middle of the conversation, so to speak?

Next, count the number of times the word "I" appears in your letter. A few are okay, but if you have too many, eliminate them by rewriting. When possible, convert "I" statements to "you" statements. Remember, your reader will be more interested in what you can do for her than what she can do for you. Here is an example of an "I" to "you" conversion:

> I have ten years of experience in pharmaceutical sales. I have existing contacts within every major hospital and clinic in the state. I know the product line, and I know what it takes to make a profit in this market.

> ✿

> You don't need a beginner in pharmaceutical sales. You want someone with years of experience, someone with existing contacts in every major hospital and clinic in the state. You want a rep who already knows your product lines. With ten years of directly related experience, I know what it takes to make a profit for you in this market.

Here is another example:

> I can be productive from the first day. I have excellent references, and I am available to help you now.

> ✿

> You want someone who can be productive from the first day, has excellent references, and is available to help you now. I can be that person for you.

Also, since cover letters are governed by the same abbreviated grammar as résumés, you can simply omit many excess "I"s. This is especially useful when applied to accomplishment statements, as in this example:

> When I came on board, I reorganized the entire department. I was able to achieve a 12% reduction in staff costs with zero loss of service.

> ✿

> Recruited to reorganize the entire department. Achieved 12% reduction in staff costs with zero loss of service.

Whenever you can write "you" or "your company" or mention the company by name, you reinforce the reader's interest and reassure her that you identify with her needs and her company.

Next, remove any jargon that your reader might not know. It is fine to use acronyms or jargon that are universally understood in your field, from the widely used—CPA, CEO, ROI, P&L, cost center—to the industry-specific—SKU (retail), PE (engineering), beta test (high tech). Avoid acronyms that are peculiar to one company or a narrow niche in a particular industry. Few readers will know that the "C5 Cluster" is a quality group within your company *unless you tell them*. If you are a design engineer appointed to the Space Suit Topographical Reconnaissance Inquiry Panel (SSTRIP), define it the first time, then just call it SSTRIP.

Be sure to edit your letter for insupportable allegations or self-congratulatory bombast. People who have to gild their accomplishments with adjectives like "outstanding," "excellent," "incredible," "astounding," and "amazing," are the opposite of impressive. Enthusiasm and zeal are appreciated, arrogance and audacity are not. No one is going to like someone who writes, "I am positive that with my outstanding background of accomplishment I can reverse Universal Diversified's disappointing entry into the gas-widget market and generate record profits," even if it's true. If you have any statements like "I'm sure that I'm the best possible candidate for this position," or "If you were so lucky as to recruit me, I could lead your division to unbelievable prosperity," perhaps you'd better rewrite them.

Next, search your letter for extraneous information—information that may be important to you, for whatever reason, but unimportant to the intended reader. Anything about your hobbies, religious or social affiliations, nonwork accomplishments, and so on is probably better left out *unless* you can relate it to your candidacy. Height, weight, age, date or place of birth, marital status, and health information should definitely be omitted. (Although some candidates believe that it's a plus to describe marital and family situations, I rarely agree.)

If any part of your letter sounds like whining or excuses, rewrite it. In particular, never say anything bad about a former employer or introduce a problem that might not have occurred to the reader. If you were fired from your last position, or you will need a month off soon to join your parents on a cruise, let it come out later, perhaps in the second or third interview.

How long should your letter be? If it's unusually long, and some executive letters are two pages or even more, then it had better be very good. The heading for all pages after the first should be the addressee's name and title, the date, and the page number, as in this heading for the second page of a letter from you to R. R. Bobbingalong:

Robert R. Bobbingalong, Director of Engineering

August 1, 1994, page 2

(letter continues here)

In general, your letter should be as short as possible. Here is a perfectly serviceable letter:

Dear Mr. Bancroft:

As you requested, you will find my résumé enclosed, in application for the position of Director, Efficiency Engineering. I will call you on Friday to answer any preliminary questions you may have. Thank you for your interest.

Sincerely,

I. M. Brief

This letter is efficient, but it doesn't add any "sell" to the résumé; Ms. Brief has missed her chance to brag about past successes and predict future contributions. You generally want to let the employer know a little about what you have done for others, and what you can do for them.

On the other hand, many job-search letters end up being quite redundant; they simply reiterate the résumés that accompany them. If you can send a good, highly targeted résumé with your letter, you can remove the discussion of past accomplishments from your rationale with no loss of impact. If you have a good heading that will allow your letter to be routed accurately, a good intro that incites reader interest, and a precise call to action that tells the reader what to do next, your letter may not need a rationale at all. If, after one pass at editing, your letter is still too long, try summarizing or omitting data from your rationale.

In general, each letter should be one page long, with large, readable type, and at least one-inch margins on every side. Be sure to proofread one last time for spelling, grammar, and stylistic consistency. You may wish to have at least one other person look it over before you mail it.

In the end your letter may have a few rough edges, but don't obsess about it. A successful job search depends not only on the *quality* of work, but also on the *quantity* of work performed. It's better to send out 100 letters with a typo in each than to send out ten that are perfect. You could have landed a great new position long before a perfectionist decides her letter is good enough to send out. Full speed ahead!

Print your letter on the same paper as your résumé. If that's not possible, use a textured white, light grey, or light tan paper, 8½ × 11 or 7¼ × 10½, and at least 24 lb. weight. If you are applying for a creative position, other colors may be appropriate. Heavy paper denotes a heavyweight candidate; and light, flimsy paper, a lightweight. Typing and word processing are both standard, but avoid using a dot-matrix printer. Unless an advertisement specifically directs you to, *never* send a handwritten business letter. (Some thank-you notes *can* be handwritten, see chapter 7, "Thank-You Letters.")

If you are sending a one-page letter by itself, use a standard #10 business envelope. If it's two or more pages long, or if you are enclosing your résumé, *do not fold up your materials.* Use a 9 × 12 envelope, either manila or white, to send everything out flat. A résumé is a marketing piece, and, as such, should not be folded up. Would you wad up a full-color brochure and send it to a prospective customer? Paper-clip the letter and résumé together (gold paper clips are a nice touch). You will need to mark 9 × 12 envelopes "First Class Mail," and be sure to pay the extra postage. You don't want your mailing to arrive late, or with postage due. Second-day or overnight delivery can often be worth the extra charges.

Congratulations! You're almost ready to mail. Even if you are trying to get that letter out tonight, though, be sure to read the chapter that describes your job-search letter's type in depth. Each chapter is short, filled with full-scale examples, and designed to let you make sure *quickly* that you've done everything you can to craft a winning letter.

The Idiot-Proof Letter

Anyone who is at the management level and does not write individual, customized letters is not serious about his job search. That said, if you do not have access to a typewriter, or any way to produce individualized cover letters, and you are too broke to buy one, then you should know about the idiot-proof cover letter. This is a form letter that you can have typed up at a copy shop or typing service, then photocopy by the hundreds and send out without changing a word. This technique will work, but use it only in emergencies. The other letters in this book will work *much* better. Just fill in the date and the intended recipients by hand and mail them out:

Sandy McKie
1602 Lancaster Lane
Baltimore, Maryland 21205
(301) 555-9348

Date: June 15, 1994
Attn: Human Resourses,
Apex, Acme, and Zenith, Inc.

Dear Prospective Employer:

In the interest of exploring employment opportunities with your organization, I have enclosed a copy of my résumé that briefly describes my qualifications and credentials.

As you can see, I have had positions of considerable responsibility. I have a reputation for dedication and quality performance. I am willing to give an assignment whatever it takes to bring it to fruitful completion.

Please consider me as a serious candidate for any position for which I may be qualified. I would like to meet with you or your designated representative to discuss your needs and how I may best contribute to your success. Please contact me to arrange an interview at your convenience.

Thank you for your consideration. I look forward to our conversation.

Respectfully yours,

Sandy McKie

Sandy McKie

Enc: Résumé

No matter what you have to work with, try to craft the best letter you can. Now you should turn to the appropriate chapter for further help with the specific type of letter you need to write. Good luck!

Chapter Three
Cover Letters for Announced Openings

Your Letter as a Routing Slip

An announced opening is one that has been advertised via a newspaper ad, trade publication, computer network, job hotline, or bulletin board. Technically, jobs listed only with headhunters are also announced openings, but this chapter will cover only those jobs that have been advertised to the general public.

You will have serious competition for any announced position. The employer will attract applications from dozens, if not hundreds, of fully qualified candidates. Your letter has to succeed in getting routed to the right person in the right office, and then screened into the "further consideration" pile. Those are two separate steps.

In the first, your cover letter serves as a routing slip for the attached résumé; its primary function is to get your résumé in front of a viable decision-maker. If your letter can be routed to that person *without its even being read,* there's a much higher chance it will make it to its intended final destination. When responding to a job announcement, place the targeted position's title, and any codes from the announcement, right in your letter's heading.

Use that handy Latin word "re" (pronounced "ray," it means "concerning"). If a contact person is given, you can also use the abbreviation "Attn" in your heading. When responding to a newspaper advertisement, include the name of the newspaper and the date the advertisement ran. (Some people actually cut out the advertisement and tape it to their letters, but that wouldn't be appropriate at the management level.) You can even use bold print to highlight the addressee and your job target, making it even easier to route your letter. Here are two examples of easy-to-route letters:

June 15, 1994

Serious Comedy
1400 Broadway, 6th Floor
New York, New York 10014

Attn: **Ulysses B. Serious**

Re: **Assistant Copywriter** (*New York Times,* 6/14/93)

Dear Mr. Serious:

(body of letter starts here)

✿

August 12, 1994

Office of the Chief Financial Officer
Ewing Oil Company, Inc.
28000 Corporate Drive
Dallas, Texas 75225

Attn: J. R. Ewing, Section Chief

Re: Senior Oil Markets Analyst, WSJ-65R, MS-218 (8/8/94)

Dear J. R. Ewing:

(body of letter starts here)

You should be advised that companies often use fake names in their ads; when you try to call "J. R. Ewing" you will be screened automatically, because J. R. Ewing is a fictional character and the company knows you are responding to the advertisement. To get around this practice, call the potential employer *before* sending in your letter and say something like this, "I heard that you were looking for a senior oil markets analyst. I think I've got a lot to offer for a position like that. Who's handling the search and to whom should I address my letter and résumé?"

When responding to an ad that specifies "No Calls," do the same thing. Call the company as if you never saw the ad, and say, "A friend of mine in the business alerted me to the fact that you may have an opening for an oil analyst. I'd like to know who's handling that search, so I can submit a cover letter and a résumé right away." Decide in advance who this friend is, because they may ask.

This technique won't always get you an accurate name, but often it will. You should also pursue multiple lines of attack, *especially* when an announcement says to send résumés to the human resources department. Get on the phone and try to identify the line manager whom the advertised position will be reporting to, then send her a cover letter and résumé as well. If you can't get a name, write to an approximate title: "Head of Oil Markets Analysis," "Chief Financial Officer," "Vice President of Marketing." You might want to try writing a note to the line manager one or two steps *above* the position you're applying for, something like this: "I heard you were looking for an oil analyst. I've enclosed my résumé for your review. If you are not managing the hiring on this placement, please forward my materials to the appropriate person." Don't be afraid to send several letters to the same company.

Before responding to an advertisement that doesn't name any employer at all, read the section below on blind box ads.

Incidentally, six-month-old want ads are an excellent source of job leads. Look for advertisements seeking managers one or two steps above you. This gives you accurate titles for recently hired managers, and such managers are always much more receptive to new ideas and staff reorganizations than the deadwood they replaced. Write to them using the techniques in chapter 5, "Broadcast Letters for Targeted Companies."

Staying in the "Yes" Pile

You must send a customized letter to each and every job announcement. Read and analyze the announcement's every nuance. Make a list of clues available in the advertisement, then try to imagine what additional skills or talents might interest this employer. Imagine what challenges might be on the horizon for the company in general, and the advertised position in particular. If you can demonstrate not only the qualifications needed to perform immediately, but the vision and where-withal for future success, you will be a strong candidate.

Next, return to the exercise described earlier; scour your entire background for concrete evidence that you possess the skills, talents, knowledge, aptitudes, and background of an ideal candidate. Consider all of your work, educational, social, volunteer, family, and leisure experiences. Much of this evidence will find its way into your letter's rationale.

"If you want to get off this deadwood short list, Oakerson, I suggest you: one, get some accounting skills; two, get some management skills; three, get some social skills; four, get real."

Reprinted by permission of Tribune Media Services

In these letters, the introduction is less important, as they're not unsolicited. As long as your letter is routed to the right desk, it will get a fair review along with everyone else's. Be sure to increase your chances by dropping the names of any pertinent networking or referral contacts. It is okay to use a simple introduction, like:

> I was very interested to learn of your need for a **Senior Staff Accountant**. My good friend Molly Rhinegold is a manager with your organization, and she has only the highest praise for the firm. My résumé is enclosed for your review.
>
> As you can see . . .

You will find many good rationale paragraphs in the previous chapter. Your main task is to make sure that each rationale is custom-crafted to match the announced job, and no other. Avoid using the table-style rationale that some books recommend, as it can only highlight your shortcomings.

Your Requirements:	My Qualifications:
*Item from Ad	*Item from Your Background
*Etc.	*Etc.

This kind of point-by-point response to a job announcement is reductionist; it eliminates subtlety and nuance, and makes it very easy for the employer to rate your background quantitatively against others who use a similar format. There will *always* be another candidate with one more year of experience or one more credential than you, and there will be many, many candidates with the minimum qualifications. You want to be the one candidate who answers the employer's unstated but implied concerns. (See the examples in the back of this chapter.)

Your call to action should be as precise as you can make it. You should call within forty-eight hours of when your letter arrives, if at all possible. And you should tell them you are going to do so.

Blind Box Ads

"Blind box ads" are help-wanted ads that do not identify the advertiser; the candidate is instructed to apply to a post office box, or in care of the newspaper. Employers run blind box ads for several perfectly good reasons: they may not want their own employees to know of impending staff changes, they may not want to give their competitors advance notice of their business plans, or they may not want their customers to worry about upcoming management changes. In addition, such employers don't have to acknowledge applications or otherwise trouble themselves with etiquette or public relations.

Some ads *do* list a street address, but no company name. An enterprising candidate can use a reverse directory or actually visit the address to identify the company. If the ad lists a post office box, you can march into the nearest post office with the advertisement in hand and say, "According to USPS Communication 352.44 'Disclosure of Names and Addresses of Customers,' Paragraph 4, 'Post office box address,' Section 1, 'Business use,' you are required to provide me with the name, address, and telephone number of this advertiser. To quote 352.44e(1): 'The recorded name, address, and telephone number of the holder of a post office box being used for the purpose of doing or soliciting business with the public . . . will be furnished to any person.'" The postmaster must comply with this regulation whether the box in question is located at that station or not, and regardless of whether it was rented by a business or an individual.

Only ads that list a newspaper box number are truly "blind." If you have reason to fear that the advertiser is your own employer, or anyone else you don't wish to contact, just prepare your application as usual, and seal it in an envelope addressed to the box number. Then place that envelope inside a second one addressed to the newspaper's mailroom, with a letter such as this:

Dear Daily Truth:

I am responding to the help-wanted advertising Box 3128 from Sunday's paper, 6/14/94. Please DO NOT FORWARD the enclosed application if the employer is Smith Linoleum or Floors-to-Roll. Thank you for your diligence in this matter.

With today's proliferation of management-level search firms and consultants, one can never be entirely sure—you might still be inadvertently applying to your own employer. Any company could be hiding behind an ad placed by "Smelte, Kline & Gubanski." However, you can do some screening of your own, using the technique illustrated in the following letter. Note that the letter is enticing, but just vague enough that it would be difficult to trace back to the principal:

Dear Advertiser:

A friend has asked me to write on her behalf concerning the position you have advertised. She is eminently qualified for this opportunity. Some of her accomplishments relative to your requirements are as follows:

- Directed sales and marketing for a start-up medical equipment manufacturing company using the same technologies mentioned in your advertisement. Facilitated the migration from R&D to full commercialization. Brought a market focus to what had been an engineering-driven company. Launched product, exceeded goals for gross and net revenues, current direct sales in range of $15 to $25 million.

- Created distributor- and product-support networks in other regions of the United States, effectively doubling gross sales with minimal increase in fixed expenses.

- Researched export markets and wrote company strategy to be implemented beginning FY1995.

- Strong technical background. Advanced degree in applied physics, undergraduate degree in mathematics, minor in business. Effective bridge between engineering and sales.

Due to my friend's prominent and critical position with her current employer, I have agreed to serve as her proxy. I am not a placement professional; I am providing this service as a professional courtesy to you both.

Please call me to arrange a confidential interview.

Sincerely,

Whata Friend

Of course, the potential employer must reveal its identity before your friend reveals yours. This is an elaborate approach, but worth it if you need to protect yourself.

Timing

If a job announcement offers a fax number, asks you to respond "immediately," or otherwise has a sense of urgency about it, respond right away. The employer may be eager to hire someone, and your prompt action could be rewarded with a job in short order. Especially at the entry- to lower-middle-management level, the hiring process may take only a few days. While you dally writing your letter and preparing your materials, someone may already be earning a salary in the position you thought you were applying for. By the way, if you do fax in your résumé, be sure also to send a hard copy by mail. This gives you two impacts for the price of one, and a backup in case the fax is less-than-readable.

On the other hand, most management-level placements are not rush jobs—a formal search usually takes a total of thirty to ninety days, or even longer, from announcement to hiring. Some savvy careerists wait until promising newspaper ads are ten days to two weeks old, to avoid looking like they are desperately answering every advertisement in the paper. Some

ment by a friend, who thought the position might be of interest to me. It certainly was. . ." If you use this technique, be prepared to name that friend in an interview situation.

The real benefit of a late response is the chance that the stack of résumés may have already been through the first round of eliminations, which can reduce your competition by as much as 90 percent or more. Obviously, this technique can also backfire; the employer may have already spoken to candidates that he finds very desirable.

Nevertheless, any new job-seeker should diligently search through the last six to eight weeks worth of want ads and apply to the appropriate ones as though they were fresh. Many of them still will be.

One employer I know made the huge mistake of discarding all the résumés he had received as soon as he thought he had "hired" a finalist. Between accepting his offer and the first scheduled day of work, the finalist decided not to take the job after all. At that point, this employer told me, he would have hired *any* viable candidate just to keep his project on schedule. As it was, no one applied late, no one called back, and his project was delayed while he started his search all over again.

Go for It

Take a look at the following examples, and also see chapter 11, "Continuing Interest Letters." Good luck!

S. Rudy Brunot
3100 Grand Avenue, Apt. 5A
Des Moines, IA 50312
Days: (515) 555-1289
Eves: (515) 555-3867

August 1, 1994

Recruiter, Interpol
Office of the Director, North American Affairs
1307 Eye Street, Dept. A-FR2132, MS 41
Washington, D.C. 20531

Re: Announcement QR-3218
     Special Investigator, North American Affairs
     Closing date: 9/1/94

Dear Recruiter:

Please accept this letter and the enclosed résumé in formal application for the
position of Special Investigator, North American Affairs.

It has been my ambition to serve a world-class investigative service for some
time now, and I learned of Interpol's North American office during my research
into careers in this area. I have read about Interpol in books, of course,
including Jesperson's Encyclopedia of Espionage and Investigative Services of
the World. A family friend who is an FBI agent also recommended that I contact
you. I called your organization and had a conversation with S. A. Giardino,
who strongly encouraged me to apply. He forwarded Annc. QR-3218 and
instructions on how to apply.

I have the following qualifications relative to your requirements:

   * B.S., Avionics, Embry-Riddle Aeronautical University, 1991.

   * U.S. citizen, born on Cyprus to English father and Cypriot mother,
      naturalized along with my parents on January 10, 1981. Currently valid
      United States passport.

   * Foreign languages: Greek (several dialects), Italian, German, Spanish
      (Mexican dialect), Portuguese. Trilingual, Greek-English-Spanish.

   * 26 years of age, excellent physical condition. Height: 6'3", weight:
      185 lbs., passed FAA Class 1 physical.

   * Trained in race-car driving (in U.S. and Europe).

   * Single-engine flight training (soloed in Cessna 150).

   * Exemplary personal background; no problems of any kind.

   * Single, career-committed, available for unlimited travel and/or
      relocation as needed.

   * Fundamental belief in the concept that the rule of law should hold over
      all citizens equally.

I have a strong technical aptitude, knowledge of automotive mechanics, basic
flight training in single-engine aircraft, basic understanding of gems and
jewelry, knowledge of personal computers, advanced knowledge of communications
electronics, and successful sales experience. I believe I could make a
significant contribution as a Special Investigator for Interpol.

Recruiter, Interpol
Office of the Director, North American Affairs
8/1/94, page 2

I have a familiarity with firearms, mainly gained from my experience as a hunter and in shooting with friends who are gun collectors. I have extensive experience with rifle and shotgun, and would welcome additional training in specialty arms.

Possibly of great advantage, I grew up trilingual, with a native accent in American English, The Queen's English, Mexican Spanish, and Cyprian Greek. I can pass for a native in these dialects. My father was an agent for a Greek shipping line, and we lived at different times in New York, Los Angeles, Cyprus, London, and Tampico.

I think of myself as a well-rounded person, and an expert in types of aircraft and communications electronics, but more importantly, knowledgeable on a wide range of subjects. I'm a news junkie, reading two or more papers daily and watching CNN for hours at a time.

Also, in my career as a consumer-electronics sales professional, I have proved that I have a knack for dealing with different types of people. People seem to be comfortable with me, and I assume that would be an asset to an investigator. (I have been offered promotions into management positions, but declined them as I knew I was leaving this field.)

Finally, I am good with paperwork. Writing reports, accurate descriptions, exact quantitative measurements, and so on, would be easy for me. When called upon to testify, I anticipate that I could present information accurately and professionally.

I am drawn to a career in investigative services because of the potential for exciting assignments, and because I think it would suit my personality. I am an independent person, most of my extended family lives far away, I am interested in peoples and cultures all over the world, and I believe I am suited to the type of career that Interpol has to offer.

You can see that I am seeking a career, not a job. Should I be selected, my commitment to Interpol will be long-term, and it is my ambition to be an exemplary investigator.

I understand that this letter is only the beginning of the process. Thank you for your consideration of these materials. I would be more than happy to provide you with any additional information that you should need immediately, and I certainly look forward to an opportunity in a personal interview to establish my desire and ability to perform on your behalf. I will call your office on Friday to confirm receipt of these materials, and to discuss the next stage of the selection process.

Again, thank you.

Sincerely,

Rudy Brunot

S. Rudy Brunot

Enclosure

Sonia E. Baker

1220 Wagon Wheel Road
Lawrence, Kansas 66049

Telephone:
(913) 555-9891

January 4, 1995

Donald K. Donaldson
Andersen, Donaldson & Associates
1446 Ethan Allen Way, Suite 100
Sacramento, California 95825
(916) 555-5575

Dear Mr. Donaldson:

I was interested to come across your advertisement in JobBANK for a Manager of Cultural Affairs for the City of Santa Monica, California. I have been seeking an opportunity such as this, and I think you will find that I might fit your job description. I have enclosed my résumé for your review.

My background is in city planning and arts administration, which has proved to be an extremely effective combination. I believe my skills, abilities, and accomplishments are represented, albeit briefly, in the enclosed materials.

In checking my background, you will find that I have succeeded in two different but equally important areas: providing effective leadership, direction, and management; and making the arts fun and participatory for a very wide range of constituents, from public school students to major benefactors. It is difficult to show "feel-good" accomplishments, but you will note that throughout my career I have been able to marshal the support, cooperation, and enthusiasm of an incredibly diverse set of peers and colleagues.

I feel that I have been instrumental in generating long-term benefits for the organizations which I have served, benefits that can best be summarized as (1) increased financial support, (2) increased public support, and (3) increased organizational efficiency.

I already have good friends in Southern California and would welcome relocation to the area. This position is of great interest to me. I think that your client, the City of Santa Monica, might be interested in my candidacy as well. Perhaps your introduction could be beneficial to all concerned.

Thank you for your attention to these materials, and I'll be calling you very soon to see if you have any questions and to discuss your selection process.

Yours sincerely,

Sonia E. Baker
Enclosures

BRENDA J. WILSON

1703 Walnut Grove Avenue
Philadelphia, Penn. 19107

Office/Voicemail: (215) 555-7983, ext. 2856
Residence/Message: (215) 555-0911

Metropolitan Children's Hospital
P.O. Box 411067
Philadelphia, Penn. 19002

August 7, 1994

Attn: Robin Boyd, Human Resources
Re: Director for Patient Financial Services

Dear Ms. Boyd:

I was very interested to see your advertisement for a Director of Patient Financial Services. I have been seeking just such an opportunity as this, and I think my background and your requirements may be a good match. My C.V. is enclosed for your review.

Of particular note for you and the members of your team as you consider this management placement are my strong accomplishments in **reducing outstandings** and **reorganizing accounting and collections functions** to achieve improved operating efficiency internally and improved cashflow for the institution as a whole.

Consider the following:
- Reduced A/R days from 110 to 60.4.
- Reduced staff by 6.5 FTEs with concurrent increase in total departmental performance.
- Reduced patient complaints with simultaneous increase in A/R collected.
- Improved cashflow by $1.6 million per month.

Additionally, my contributions have mainly been achieved by improving information flow within the patient financial services function, improving patient financial services utilization of already available MIS services, and improving cooperation between patient services and admissions, UR, contracting, and medical records functions.

After fifteen years in patient accounting, I have a thorough understanding of every aspect of this function in a modern hospital/medical center setting. My current employer is very happy with my performance, but I view myself as somewhat of a troubleshooter, and most of the reorganizations initiated here have already come to fruition, so I am eager to consider new challenges.

If you are seeking a manager who stays abreast of her field, who understands technology, who earns 100% staff support, and who is as career-committed as it takes to achieve total success, then please consider what I have to offer. I would be happy to have a preliminary discussion with you or members of your committee to see if we can establish a mutual interest. I will call you within the week to answer any initial questions you may have, and to hear about your hiring process.

Thank you for your attention to these materials. I certainly look forward to exploring this further.

Yours sincerely,

Brenda J. Wilson

Brenda J. Wilson

Enclosure

Dorothy E. Bromo
2930 Marigold Fields, #32
Richmond, California 94805
(510) 555-2277

January 31, 1995

Bond, Bratson & Brandini
100 Bancroft Way
Berkeley, California 94710

Attn: Wallace Brown/Hiring Partner
Re: Communication Specialist/Administrative Assistant

Dear Mr. Brown:

In this modern world there is a new model for a successful career—a series of lateral moves that keeps a person involved in new tasks while using the same set of skills. The worker gets the satisfaction of variety, and of doing something well, and the employer gets the benefit of an employee with extensive related experience.

When I saw your advertisement for a communication specialist/administrative assistant, I was very interested. With international experience, a background in marketing and communications, and industry knowledge of health-care and medicine, I think there is good potential for a match. Finally, given my educational background, I am sure I can learn any and all industry-specific terminology and practices rather quickly.

Having long been interested in the legal field, I think this position could be a very beneficial long-term move for me. If you are interested in a lot of talent and experience, and you can offer challenge and opportunity to contribute, then I am sure we can come to terms.

May I be so assertive as to ring you and ask for an interview? I will call to follow up this Friday before noon, and I hope to speak with you or your designated representative then.

Thank you for your consideration. I look forward to our conversation.

Sincerely,

Dorothy E. Bromo

Dorothy E. Bromo

Enclosure: Résumé

This letter gives an excellent rationale for a lateral move. This candidate applied for a support position and ended up being hired into a $70,000 executive slot.

E. Edleff Bloader

4 White Street, 5R
New York, NY 10012
(212) 555-4438

---

11 September 1994

Donald J. A. Watkins, Ph.D.
Acting Vice President for Public Affairs
Reed College
Portland, OR 97202

Dear Dr. Watkins:

Please accept this letter and the enclosed curriculum vitae in preliminary application for the position of Director of Development at Reed College.

I learned of the opening from a Reed alumnus here in New York. He was enthusiastic about the possibility of a good fit between my background and strengths and Reed's needs at this time. After a brief discussion with your President's office, I was advised to forward my c.v. to you immediately. I understand that you are formulating a position announcement, and I would appreciate a copy as soon as it is ready. I will forward additional materials as may be specified in the announcement.

As I understand them, the challenges facing Reed are not unlike the ones I faced when I first took over as CEO of the Coron Foundation. Coron's program had an exemplary reputation, but the foundation had faced a series of organizational and funding difficulties. My goal was, above all, to maintain and protect the integrity of Coron's fellowship program and its reputation as an academic foundation of the first rate. At the same time, I needed to increase the financial strength of the institution and improve the morale and emotional commitment of key staff members.

As my curriculum vitae will indicate, we more than succeeded.

It would be my greatest pleasure to make a similar contribution to Reed College. I believe that an institution of Reed's caliber has unique development opportunities, and it is precisely because of the strength of Reed's program that I am drawn to apply.

I will call you within a few days to follow up on this letter and to discuss the selection criteria and process with you personally. Whether we do indeed find a good fit, I very much look forward to discussing Reed's development program in greater detail with you and other members of the search committee.

Thank you for your assistance.

Sincerely,

E. Edleff Bloader

E. Edleff Bloader

Enclosure
EEB/da

JEANNA H. FINE

2548 Sutter Street
San Francisco, California 94109

Telephone/Message:
(415) 555-1514

March 3, 1993

Attn: Mr. Peter North
Director of Fine Arts
Butterup & Butterup
220 San Bruno Avenue
San Francisco, California 94103

Dear Mr. North:

Thank you so much for your kind words and your encouraging me to apply for the position of California American specialist with Butterup & Butterup.

As you will remember, I have three years of full-time experience as an early-California painting specialist with the Maxwell Galleries here in San Francisco, where I have benefited from having the independent responsibility for researching artists, schools, and paintings. I have been keeping abreast of the market since 1984, have a strong ability to access and retain art information, and wide-ranging experience encompassing the Southern and Northern California Plein Aire schools (Guy Rose, Joseph Raphael, Edgar Payne, Granville Redmond, et al.) and American Realist landscape painters from 1850 on (Albert Bierstadt, Thomas Hill, William Keith, William Coulter, et al.), just to name a few.

I am currently working part-time at Maxwell Galleries, and have excellent local references to attest to my knowledge and my ability to work well with collectors. Of particular interest to a house such as Butterup & Butterup is my ability and willingness to research and learn new artists, disciplines, schools, and styles. I have my own library of art books which will assist me for quick reference, and I am eager to see your library, which I anticipate would be quite extensive.

If you would be so kind as to meet with me to discuss this position, I would be most appreciative. Thank you for your consideration, and I look forward to our next conversation.

Yours sincerely,

Jeanna H. Fine

Jeanna H. Fine

Enclosure

Victoria Welles

13 Redwood Lane
Crescent City, CA 96412
(707) 555-3543

April 30, 1995

Attn: James Chee, Investigator
Re: **Investigator**

Office of the Attorney General
State of New Mexico
6301 Indian School Road NE
Albuquerque, New Mexico 87109

Dear Mr. Chee:

It is my understanding that your office is currently interviewing candidates for a position as **investigator** with your office. I have been seeking just such an opportunity as this, and would appreciate consideration for the opening. Attached please find a copy of my résumé, briefly describing my skills, experience, and contributions on behalf of organizations such as your own. Since you are already interviewing, I want to stress that I can be available in New Mexico at your earliest convenience.

As a police officer in Eureka, California, I performed field investigations of a complete range of misdemeanors and felonies from petty theft to rape. Because this was a town of 25,000, I was responsible for investigating crimes, lifting and matching prints, collecting and preserving physical evidence, coordinating with forensics and other laboratories, and working up cases for the District Attorney's office. I have always taken great pride in my knowledge of law and rules of evidence, and not one single case I worked on had even one piece of evidence rejected on grounds of rules of evidence.

Since leaving the police department, my background has included experience investigating fraud, auto theft, embezzlement, and other white-collar crimes, as well as the usual felony investigations. Some of these cases have been politically sensitive, and others have required the ability to sustain a clandestine investigation over a period of time (embezzlement and fraud cases). My strengths include "paper" cases, the evaluation of large volumes of documentary evidence, and interrogations, interviews, and "gut-level" evaluation of cases. My record is exemplary, with significant responsibility for strategizing case investigations and coordinating others on the case.

Incidentally, prior to this I served as a fingerprint examiner for the California Department of Justice for over two years. This experience could be of use to you. Currently I am on the crime-scene technical staff, photographing, videotaping, measuring, and diagraming crime scenes.

I certainly appreciate your consideration of this application. I will call you Monday, May 3, 1995, before noon to discuss this further. It would be an honor and a privilege to serve the State of New Mexico, and I look forward to our conversation.

Sincerely,

Victoria Welles

Victoria Welles

Chapter Four
Networking Letters

Networking Everybody You Have Ever Met in Your Entire Life

Early in your job search, it is a good idea to let everyone you know in on the fact that you are considering seeking another position. Each person you contact becomes another link in your network; their eyes and ears will serve as your eyes and ears, picking up job leads for you from coast to coast. Before you send out any networking letters, make exhaustive lists of people you can contact regarding your search. As mentioned in chapter 1, your lists should include:

- Family members
- Friends
- Acquaintances
- Employers, former employers, coworkers, and former coworkers
- Clients and customers of current or former employers
- Vendors, suppliers, and business partners
- Classmates, professors, and teachers
- Club and association members
- Members of your church, temple, mosque, or ashram
- Neighbors and former neighbors

Once you have these lists of names (leads), divide each one into **hiring authorities** (people who could actually give you a job if they wanted to), **direct referral sources** (people who could personally refer you to a hiring authority), and **indirect referral sources** (everybody on the planet who doesn't fall into one of the first two categories).

In general, use the techniques in chapter 5, "Broadcast Letters for Targeted Companies," to approach hiring authorities. Approach direct referral sources with a networking letter like the ones you will find in this chapter, but *be sure to call them back regularly for the duration of your job search*. Call indirect referral sources at least once, within a week after they receive your networking letter.

Networking letters won't work unless you have a clear job objective. You cannot just write to people saying, "Gosh, Uncle Bob, if you hear about any sort of job opening, I'd sure appreciate it if you would give me a call." You need to let Uncle Bob know precisely what you're looking for:

> I'm looking for a position in tribology, which is the science of friction, lubrication, and wear. If you know of anybody at a mechanical engineering firm, or an industrial or manufacturing plant, I'd sure appreciate the lead. I'll contact them directly about potential jobs in tribology. Really rack your brains for me, Uncle Bob, because tribology is kind of an obscure field and I'll need all the help I can get. Thanks.

Here's an example seeking a broader type of job objective:

> As you know, my entire history has been in food manufacturing. I am looking for a new challenge, perhaps a young company seeking a period of rapid growth, or a more mature company that needs a firm hand at the wheel to engineer some downsizing and cost-containment, whether in a particular department, division, or functional area of a larger company, or companywide for a smaller concern. I'll ring you sometime next week to see if this letter conjures up any ideas that might be of use to me in my search.
>
> Thank you for your help, and if you ever need a return favor, count on me anytime.

Be sure to be explicit about your request for ideas, leads, and referrals:

> I think it's likely that one of your friends, or possibly someone in your own company, may be interested in someone with my background. I'll give you a call next week to see if you have any ideas, leads, or referrals for me.

> ✿

> Since you know the quality of my work, would you take a moment and consider who might be interested in what I have to offer? I'll be calling you soon to see if you have any suggestions for me. In the meantime, my best wishes as always.

Do let the recipient know that you are not applying to *her* for a job. This nice touch is called "lowering the ante," and it will make your contacts more willing to help. Remember, you are looking for a good fit, not just any old job that you can find anywhere. This example lower's the ante in a couple of paragraphs:

> At this time I am not applying for a particular position, rather I am interested in discussing opportunities and possible career paths with you, in light of your knowledge of the industry. With this in mind, I would greatly appreciate a moment of your time to discuss your company and others you might be able to recommend.

> Thank you for your attention to this letter and the enclosed materials. I will be calling you shortly to follow up on this mailing. I am eager to hear what ideas, leads, or referrals you may be able to come up with. I look forward to our conversation.

Consider sending extra résumés with any networking letter. Of course, if you are still employed, twice before empowering your old choir director to spread your résumés all over town. A paragraph like these can encourage your contacts to market you:

> I have enclosed a few copies of my résumé. Please feel free to forward them to any appropriate parties, either inside or outside your company. I appreciate your assistance, and I'll call you next week to follow up.

> ✿

> I am also enclosing a few copies of my résumé. I'd be happy to hear any feedback on it that you might be willing to give, and please feel free to forward them to anyone who might be interested. I'll ring you this Friday to hear what you think.

If you belong to a professional association, call up that association's headquarters today, buy a roster or a set of labels for the entire membership (prices vary), and send each and every one a letter something like this:

> Dear Colleague:

> As a fellow member of the Skydiving and Parachute Lovers' Association of Texas (SPLAT), I thought you might know of someone who could use a good pilot. I have six years of experience as a jump instructor and I have had a pilot's license since 1974. I'm looking for a club or a school that needs a good local pilot who not only understands skydiving, but has a passion for it. Please call me with any ideas, leads, or referrals, or, for your convenience, I've also enclosed a stamped, self-addressed postcard in case you'd rather just jot me a note. Thanks for your help.

In general, networking cover letters should be short and sweet and should close by saying that you will call to follow up, unless it's just not possible. Longer letters can be typed on standard 8½ × 11 stationery; shorter ones on monarch (7¼ × 10½) or even note-size (5½ × 8½) stationery. Do *not* write any letters by hand unless your networking contact is an intimate friend.

Go for It

In addition to the examples above, take a look at the following full-page models. Good luck!

Howard G. Bender

1638 Waterloo Street
Los Angeles, California 90026

Telephone/Message: (213) 555-0218
Fax: (213) 555-0267

July 31, 1994

Rolly W. Cabel-Teevee
Producer
Mighty Hour of Local Power
Channel 39
24596 Wilshire Boulevard
Los Angeles, California 90036

Dear Rolly:

We haven't spoken in a while, so I'm forwarding a résumé to update you on my
recent activities. I've left Jon Waters Associates and taken a short sabbatical
in Belize. I will be returning to Los Angeles soon, however, and will be
seeking a position.

Since you know of the quality of my work, would you take a moment and consider
who might be interested? Of course, I want to be V.P. to God, but I would not
be adverse to any good opportunity. I'll be calling you soon to see if you have
any suggestions. In the meantime, my best wishes as always.

Thanks for your help.

Sincerely,

Howard G. Bender

Howard G. Bender

Enclosure

Edward D. "Ted" Whittle

19 Beach Lane
Panama City, Florida 33401

Telephone/Message:
(813) 555-2864

_____

September 5, 1994

Makhijani Mahesh, Ph.D.
V.P., Marketing & Customer Engineering
Mars Telecom, Inc.
Pittsburgh, Pennsylvania 15222

Dear Dr. Mahesh:

I got your name from P. Khosrovi, who spoke very highly of you. I am interested in your industry, and I wonder if you would take a moment to speak with me as a professional courtesy.

After years of success in sales, marketing, distributor relations, product development, and new-product launch, I have begun to suspect that I may be in the wrong field. My company loves me, and I have a highly competitive compensation structure for my field, but I have friends who are doing better without even making major contributions to their employer.

At this time I am interested in learning about your industry, especially what the most viable career paths are within your field, and maybe hearing a few stories about what it takes to get into and succeed in your arena. My first preference would be a quick after-work meeting, coffee or a drink is on me. I will be in Pittsburgh next week, September 12-16, and I'll give you a call then. If you are simply too busy to arrange a meeting, perhaps we can just chat on the phone.

I have enclosed my résumé so you can get an idea of where I am coming from. (Don't worry—I'm not applying for a job. I just thought you might like to take a glance at it.)

I am eager to learn more about your company, your products, and how you go to market. In return, I will share with you what I have learned from others in similar meetings.

Thank you for your consideration.

Yours sincerely,

Edward D. "Ted" Whittle

Edward D. "Ted" Whittle

Enclosure: résumé

Chapter Five
Broadcast Letters for Targeted Companies

Your ½-Second to Win Your Reader's Attention

Unsolicited direct mail has a survival duration of about a half second. If you do not get your reader's attention in that half second, she is not likely to read further. Fortunately for you, an unsolicited letter from an individual gets far more attention than the average piece of junk mail. At least your letter will be opened. Fully a third of the mail received by some offices goes directly into the wastebasket unopened.

So what can you do in half a second to get your reader's attention? Imagine that reader cutting open your letter. She has a stack of mail to sort. She's busy. The phone's ringing. She's just spilled coffee on her keyboard, so her day's already ruined. Now she opens your letter. What is she thinking with all her heart? Answer: "Should I throw this away or what?"

If you can write an opening that she will find interesting or entertaining, or that hits one of her business hot buttons, she'll read your letter. If not, she'll throw it out or send it to personnel, which amounts to the same thing.

Remember the openings presented in chapter 2, "Components of Compelling Job-Search Letters" (see p. 9). Here they are again, roughly in order of effectiveness:

you asked for it

personal referral

hook line

news commentary

let me keep this exceedingly brief

Think of yourself as an ad writer, trying your best to win the half-second wars. (*Do not write an unsolicited letter* to a company without reading chapter 2.) Here are some more openings to consider:

On my tombstone they can write, "The man could do radio."

Your time is valuable—too valuable to spend doing the kind of organizational, administrative, and copywriting functions that I could do for you.

You know a bargain when you see one. You know that if you could get a seasoned professional for the price of a recent college graduate, you'd think it was a pretty good deal.

I was very excited by your encouragement on the phone about positions working with youths and children at Club Med. As we discussed . . .

Sure, you'd like more business. You know it's out there, and you deserve to have it, but how can you bring that new business in without spending $4 to make $5?

Before you throw this letter away, give me 30 seconds to tell you why you might like to meet me.

Everyone knows that the credit-card market is maturing fast, with more and more players chasing the same creditworthy 13 million households. There are some keys to success, however, and when I heard about your company's plans, I thought, "What a great opportunity!" I'll tell you why in just a moment.

When I started in the club business in Manhattan, my friends all said, "You're crazy! You'll never make it! You're a business person, what do you know about clubs?" Well, I knew enough to start two of the most successful clubs in recent history, and I did it precisely because I *am* a business person and not a club person.

Your corporate security is probably run on a reactive basis. Something awful happens, and someone from security is sent over to investigate and fix the blame. How would you like it if I could show you how to turn your security operations into a profit center? That's right, money back on every dollar spent.

Your customers don't know you. They only know the person who answers the phone.

Triple-digit growth. Who wouldn't like to have a little more triple-digit growth?

When it comes to your own department, isn't it nice to have a good candidate in the wings at all times? When you need someone, you usually don't have six weeks to launch a search and deal with hundreds of candidates. You want good qualified help, and you want it fast!

Are you just about ready to kill your MIS manager?

Boring cover letters get tossed out or routed into a black hole, never to be seen again. You don't want to sound immature or flaky, but you *should* take a risk with your letter, show a little creativity, sound like you might be fun to meet. Compare the above with this:

In the interest of exploring employment opportunities with your organization, I have enclosed my résumé for your review.

So what? Who cares?

Here's one last creative opening for you to consider:

Retail—Exclusive clothier seeks knowledgeable, enthusiastic sales associate. F/T. Experience essential. Must excel in both sales and customer relations. If you possess these qualities, send résumé to Polo Ralph Lauren, 90 Post St., SF, 94102.

Dear Mr. Thorton:

It would be great if I were responding to an ad like this instead of writing you an unsolicited letter. Unfortunately, I haven't seen such an ad in the *Chronicle* recently. Nevertheless, I am submitting this application because I earnestly believe that my qualifications are well suited to your store.

Offer Enthusiasm and Flexibility

When you contact a company out of the blue, you are applying for a position that may not even exist. Acknowledge this in your letter one way or another, so the employer doesn't think you are going to hound him for something he cannot provide. What he *can* provide are leads, advice, counsel, and consideration. What he *can't* provide is a job if he doesn't have one. Give him every opportunity to say yes to you. For example:

May we meet briefly to discover if we have a mutual interest? Even if you don't need anyone right away, I'd still like to meet for a brief conversation. Perhaps something will come up, and you'll already know of my skills, or perhaps you will think of a friend who could use my services sooner.

As you conduct your job search, don't be rigid about the kind of position you are seeking. A full-scale job search should also be a learning mission. No matter how savvy you are when you start, you will soon be inundated with new information. Rigid dedication to a specific objective is almost always a job-search error. Although you *do* need to have a good idea of what you want before you can contact an employer, you should always consider tangential positions and new ideas, suggestions, and opportunities as they present themselves.

In particular, consider more than the standard full-time, permanent positions. Recent research suggests that a very large percentage of all new jobs are *contingent,* that is, they are part-time, temporary, contract, or consulting assignments.

(There is a great deal of confusion about how to count these jobs, so research often yields conflicting data. Nevertheless, the numbers are huge. At least one-third, and as much as two-thirds, of all new jobs are *at least initially* contingent. Whether you want a contingent position or not, you cannot afford to ignore such a large segment of the market. Nor is this contingent-jobs phenomenon confined to lower-level positions—as companies thin their management ranks, they find they need *contingent* managers at all levels. Finally, when and if a contingent job is converted to a permanent position, the incumbent has a decided advantage in being converted along with the job.)

You can demonstrate your flexibility right off by not applying for a traditional job in the first place. Instead, tell companies that you want to "explore ways in which my background might be of benefit to your organization," or, alternately, an "opportunity to contribute to the success of your company." Remember, initially you want a discussion, not a job. Here's a high-level example:

> I am not necessarily seeking a permanent position with you. I just finished an engagement as an interim CFO with another company and have done considerable consulting in the past. Since there are many ways in which I could benefit Xericon, perhaps it would be best if we had an exploratory discussion to see if we can find a fit. I'll give you a call next week.

Employers tell me they are sick of candidates who want a job, but don't want to work. If you, on the other hand, can back up a statement like the following, you will definitely garner extra attention:

> It would be my pleasure to work **any hours** and **any shift**, including **unlimited overtime** as needed in order to establish my value to you.

Managers need to demonstrate that they can work smart as well as hard, but this sort of statement has proved extremely effective for nonexempt employees.

Think about every query from the employer's point of view. In general, decision-makers are loathe to meet with anyone who's desperate for a job, and will be relatively eager to meet with someone who seems engaging, and genuinely interested in listening to their advice. Everyone loves to talk about himself. Think about it. By *not* applying for a position before you even know if there is one, you are "lowering the ante" for your first conversation with a targeted employer.

> Can you spare a few minutes to have a short face-to-face meeting with me? I'd like to discuss career opportunities in sales in your industry. Even if you aren't planning any staff adjustments yourself any time soon, I'd still like to meet with you and hear how you got into the business, who's hot and who's not, and what ideas, leads, or suggestions you might have for someone like me.

Use a Forceful Call to Action

An unsolicited letter needs an exceedingly strong call to action. Remember, your reader is still trying to decide, "Should I throw this away or what?" You can get her to leave it on her desk by promising that she'll need it within two days. (Any longer than that and she's going to have to put it somewhere else.) Note the call to action samples in chapter 2. Here are two more:

> I'll call you on Thursday before noon. You can count on me to be prompt. If you are not in on Thursday morning, please advise your secretary as to when would be a better time for me to call.

Thank you for your consideration, and I look forward to our conversation.

✿

I will call you within 48 hours of your receipt of this mailing, so please keep my résumé handy. Thank you for your consideration, and I look forward to speaking with you soon.

Consider Using a Response Card

Some candidates really embrace the direct-mail analogy, going so far as to provide direct-response cards. These cards allow the recipient to choose one of several response options, a strategy that has proven effective in direct-mail advertising. In short, the more ways you offer a recipient to respond, the more likely it is that she *will* respond.

In addition, a postcard lets the recipient clear you off her desk by putting you in touch with the right decision-maker. Nothing could be better.

The postcard should be stamped and self-addressed. Don't forget to note the recipient on each card—the job-seeker's worst nightmare is getting back a potentially great lead and realizing that there's no clue as to who sent it to you.

Here is a model for the postcard:

Dear (Your Name Here):   From: *Amalgamated Widget, Inc.*

☐ Yes, give me a call   ☐ Call the main number

☐ My direct line/extension is:

OR   _____

☐ I have forwarded your résumé to:

Name: _____

Title: _____

Please deal with him/her directly.

Now your letter recipient has four options: she can ignore you entirely, call you, wait for your call, or deflect you by filling out the postcard. Three out of four possible responses will help your job search.

If you want to learn more about response cards, read William Frank's *200 Letters for Job-Hunters,* which has several excellent variations on this technique.

At the Executive Level, Write to a Company Officer's Secretary

An executive secretary's one and only interest is protecting her boss. She screens his mail and calls to keep out unsolicited pests like you. On the other hand, if you can appeal directly to that loyalty you will win an ally in your job search. To do this, you need to give that executive secretary a sound, rational reason that your missive will be of interest to her boss.

First of all, find out the secretary's name by calling the company's main receptionist and asking for it. *Get the correct spelling, title, and office address.* Prepare a regular letter to the executive, and then write a separate letter just for the secretary. Address your entire mailing to the secretary directly. Secretaries don't get much mail addressed directly to them, so your letter will stand garner extra attention.

This is a particularly effective technique when you are applying at the level of officer or department head. The only person qualified to review your query letter will be a higher-level officer, and that person is very unlikely to ever see your letter unless you have a direct connection.

This example is plain, but it worked immediately for the candidate who sent it:

Robert G. Daning
334A Echo Park Avenue
Los Angeles, California 90036
(213) 555-2834 or (213) 555-9103

24 April 1994

Ms. Rita Cole
Executive Assistant to the President
Pony Express & Company
120 Montgomery Street
San Francisco, California 94103

Dear Ms. Cole:

The enclosed is a letter of inquiry concerning purchasing operations at Pony Express in light of the merger with Calhoun & McCoy. It also includes a résumé of my career.

I realize that your normal procedure is probably to insulate Mr. Hazen from employment applications and to forward the enclosed directly to personnel.

Please consider that in this case he may wish to review my letter himself, as the rationale I am presenting is politically sensitive, and is one that only he could implement.

My experience as Vice President & Head of Purchasing at Chemical Bank should be of direct interest to him.

Finally, the material is brief and to the point. He will know almost immediately whether he is interested in further contact with me.

I thank you for your consideration in these matters, and I hope you will present the enclosed to Mr. Hazen for his review.

Sincerely yours,

Robert G. Daning

Don't Forget to Approach Smaller Businesses

This sort of unsolicited direct contact can be the backbone of a sophisticated, systematic job search. Be sure not to neglect smaller companies, even tiny little start-ups. Most of the new jobs being created in America today are in small- to medium-size companies. If you have never worked for a small company before, now is the time to consider it.

It's true that they provide little security and that achieving rapid career advancement may entail changing companies fairly often, but small- to medium-size companies are also easy to approach, more open to people making career transitions, *and they have jobs*. Besides, no sector of the economy is truly secure anymore. In this last wave of layoffs, companies that had staked their reputations on "permanent employment" laid off thousands and thousands.

You may also want to consider researching companies that began operations in the past year or two. Incorporation, partnership, and fictitious-business-name filings are a matter of public record. You can get the names and sometimes even the home addresses of principals and officers in small companies, then write to them offering your services. If they have been successful, they will be suffering growing pains. They will badly need financial, administrative, computing, and sales help, but they'll be too busy to launch and manage a proper search. Then your letter arrives, offering a solution to their woes.

Go for It

Take a look at the following examples, each one a little different. Be sure to note the last example in this chapter, which is one of the most original job-search letters I have ever seen. Your letters may not be so bold, but all of these are good models to work from. Good luck!

J ROBERT BLOOM

25 Divisadero Place
San Francisco, California 94115

Office direct line: (415) 555-6200
Residence: (415) 555-5200
Fax: (415) 555-7200

September 1, 1994

Attn: Andrea Miskow, Division President
Ardmore Housewares Corp.
2219 China Basin, Bldg. H-218
San Francisco, California 94112

Dear Ms. Miskow:

Are you tired of excuses? Do your top managers blame foreign competition, lazy workers, Bill Clinton, and a punitive tax structure for a lack of profits? You don't have to listen to this kind of negativity.

In my last operating position, I created a 15% increase in gross revenues in an industry that was experiencing a 30% decline. The company had a mature product line, encroaching foreign competition, a management team in disarray, and still we resolved these problems to add 15% to gross and 5.3% to margins.

In my current position, I have set up national account relationships between major companies that had not previously been business partners, generating millions of dollars in new business. In short, I can approach your business problems from both sides, i.e., creating greater profits through attention to both revenues and cost containment.

If you'd rather hear positive ideas than excuses, then let's have a "get acquainted" discussion. It won't cost you anything, and it could lead to the type of management you really want.

I'll call your office within 24 hours of your receipt of this letter. Please advise your secretary to expect my call. Thank you for your consideration, and I certainly look forward to our conversation.

Sincerely,

J Robert Bloom

J Robert Bloom

Enclosure
JRB/da

ANGELA K. BARRON

1022 Lakeshore Drive, Apt. 2C
Chicago, IL 60606

Office: (312) 555-1453
Residence: (312) 555-6461

May 7, 1995

Térèse Lawler
Sales Director, Pharmaceuticals
Chase & Chase, Inc.
1 Chase Plaza
Madison, Wisc. 53012

Dear Ms. Lawler:

"Why aren't you in sales?" If I had a dollar for every time somebody asked me that, I wouldn't need to be in sales!

Every time I orchestrate a really difficult admission, calming the patient, reining in a distraught and meddling family, finding and motivating the right resident, and then convincing some insurance carrier to bend the rules "just this once," one of my coworkers will ask, "Why aren't you in sales?"

My friends are always asking me this. "You're so pushy and nice at the same time! Why aren't you in sales?"

My answer, really, was that I wanted to learn more. Because of my sales records I could have pursued a career in retail with Macy's, but I didn't think that would be intellectually interesting enough. Now that I've completed my undergraduate degree and accumulated considerable basic knowledge—both in school and on the job—I have decided to pursue a longstanding interest in combining my education, experience, interpersonal strengths, and ambition in one arena: pharmaceutical sales.

I am not applying for a particular position with you at this time. I am just interested in learning more about your company and hearing what ideas and suggestions you may have for me. If we do discover a mutual interest, I'll make a formal application later.

On Thursday before noon I will call to follow up on this letter, so please keep this information handy. I appreciate your consideration, and I look forward to speaking with you personally.

Sincerely,

Angela K. Barron

Enclosure: résumé

Randall West

2013 Waterton Avenue
Cambridge, Massachusetts 02213

Telephone/24-hour Message:
(617) 555-8039

December 3, 1994

Mina Miyagi
Production Coordinator
Littledove & Klein
97 High Street
Suite 210
Boston, MA 02115

Dear Ms. Miyagi:

They told me I was crazy when I first went to work as a professional piano tuner for Pro-Piano in Boston. A friend who knew the company told me, "You won't make it a week."

That was nine years ago.

Concert artists are famous for being perfectionists, and it is a reputation well earned. My friend knew that nobody had been able to survive more than a few months, at most, at Pro-Piano because of the demands of the artists for perfection.

I provide perfection every day, tuning pianos to fine aesthetic standards, tuning each one three or four times for each performance. During ten minutes of intermission, I can make the piano conform to the artist's desires.

Although I am well known in my current field, there is no room for advancement. Now I want to learn your business, which is more complex and multifaceted, and in which I could advance to a higher level.

A piano tuner is the tool of the artist. I have no ego, only a desire to do my job to perfection, and an ability to use a technical skill with creativity to achieve an artistic end. Sound familiar?

If I can tune pianos for concert artists, I can serve your needs in post-production. I am available for any shift, for contract work, for travel, on any basis, you name it. My initial interest is telecine operation, but my eventual goal is to be a master colorist.

I would greatly appreciate a moment of your time. Could you spare five minutes to discuss this with me in person? I am eager to hear your ideas.

Sincerely,

Randall West

Randall West

/rw

L. Nina de Ponca

33 Lonestar Circle
Dallas, Texas 75221

Telephone/Message:
(214) 555-3260

July 13, 1994

James Lee Horner
Campaign Manager, Richards in '96
13 Commerce Square, Suite 96
Dallas, Texas 75011

Dear Mr. Horner:

Suppose someone were to offer you a cash donation of more than $30,000. That would certainly garner some attention, wouldn't it?

Suppose someone were to call offering your candidate twenty minutes of free electronic media, national, with an entirely positive slant. You'd return that call, right?

I think what I have to offer you is of equal value. Consider the following:

I am contacting you to offer my services gratis on behalf of Governor Richards' 1996 presidential campaign. At the ripe old age of 30, I accepted a highly favorable retirement offer from my corporate employer. I am using this money to fund a career transition into politics. I am available full-time, 24 hours a day, for the duration of the campaign.

However, after a fast-track career in the corporate environment, I do not want to start on your phone bank. If you will take advantage of what I have to offer, I will give you 110%. If you are not able to really utilize my talents, then perhaps you can recommend someone who can.

Here is some of my background:

Highlights

- Extensive special-project management experience involving team building, delegation, and rapid decision-making in an environment where errors are costly ($$$).

- Speech writing, newsletter editing, and other writing for internal/external distribution.

- Policies and procedures manual development involving all phases from strategic/operations analysis through regulatory compliance to hands-on management of writing and production.

- Recruiting experience, including outreach to colleges and universities.

- Heavy technical/analytical skills, report writing, policy analysis, and similar.

James Lee Horner, Campaign Manager
July 13, 1994, page 2

I am interested in a campaign position that requires ability to juggle a large volume of simultaneous responsibilities, involves exposure to the inner workings of a campaign, and entails a strong combination of people skills and, optionally, financial/analytical skills. My goal is to prove my skills on your behalf at no cost to you and later use that proof to obtain paid political consulting or campaign assignments.

Do you have a few minutes to talk about a $30,000 contribution to Governor Richards' campaign?

I'll be calling you this Thursday at 10:00 A.M. sharp. If you are not going to be available at that time, please advise Jeannette as to when would be a better time to reach you.

Thank you for your consideration of my offer. I am very excited by the opportunity to assist you.

Sincerely,

L. Nina de Ponca

L. Nina de Ponca

Enclosure: Résumé

STEPHANIE B. KOSMOS

WEST COAST:
2103 Courtney Avenue
Seattle, WA 98101
(206) 555-4316

EAST COAST:
531 Lafayette Blvd., #7B
Chapel Hill, NC 27103
(919) 555-5959

4 March 1994

Norman Vanamee
Managing Editor
New York Magazine
753 Second Avenue
New York, NY 10017

Dear Mr. Vanamee:

If energy, youth, and vitality were all I had to offer you, I probably wouldn't even bother writing this letter.

If my liberal arts education, solid understanding of the mechanics of English, and ability to make myself understood in speaking or in writing were all I had to offer you, I probably wouldn't even get out of bed in the morning.

If my understanding of both the economic and cultural issues surrounding modern magazine publishing were all I had to offer you, I'd probably just throw myself into the nearest poorhouse for the rest of my life.

What I do have to offer you, what makes me get out of bed, write you, and eschew depression and despair, is my enthusiasm for magazine publishing and my excitement at the possibility of having a summer internship with you in 1994.

You can count on me. You can count on me to call you soon to discuss this further.

Yours most respectfully,

Stephanie B. Kosmos

Stephanie B. Kosmos

/sk

HEIDI M. RUIZ

671 Peachtree Street, #7   Office/Voicemail: (706) 555-0455
Athens, Georgia 30051   Residence/Message: (706) 555-0335

February 17, 1995

B. J. Little
V.P., Sales
Chironex Corporation
171 Sherman Place, Suite 113
Atlanta, GA 30302

Dear B. J. Little:

It's not really true that I can walk on water, although perhaps some of my former employers will tell you that I can. Here are some examples of what I've been able to do for them:

- Created a $320,000 account base, starting from zero.

- Doubled the size of an existing account base.

- Personally opened 71% of a company's total account base.

- Consistently ranked #1 or #2 in the nation.

My success is based upon a simple fact: My accounts like me. They know I'll take care of them. Sometimes I think they buy my products whether they need them or not, and actually, that's why I'm writing to you today.

I need to have a product I know is NUMBER ONE, the absolute best in the field. If you want a representative who can make things happen, win and keep key accounts, and you have an outstanding product that the medical world needs to know more about, then let's get together. I'm ready to deliver a miracle.

Actually, I can walk on water, and so can you. (All you need is a frozen pond.)

I'll be calling you within 24 hours. Please keep this letter handy, and we'll chat then.

Yours sincerely,

Heidi M. Ruiz

Heidi M. Ruiz

Enclosure: résumé

SAMUEL M. VIGIL

1111 Duval Drive, Rear Cottage
Las Vegas, Nevada 89170

Telephone/message:
(702) 555-4996

December 13, 1994

Attn: John Booth, Jeff Long, Joe Perrera
Cost-Co Regional Administrative Headquarters
48103 North Bay Front Drive
Richmond, California 94804-5879

Gentlemen:

Your customers deserve to shop in a store they like. They want to know that they are getting the best deal for the price, but they also want to feel that store employees care about them, and store policies are consistent and fair.

At the same time, your employees deserve to work for managers whom they respect. They want to feel that the manager leads by example, and is willing to put in any extra effort it may take to present a well-merchandised and efficiently operated store.

I'd like to discuss with you the type of commitment I've brought to my career to date, and the type of store I want to present to customers, and the type of management I want to represent to employees. My staffs have always had high morale, low turnover, and minimal shrinkage. In spite of my contributions, I feel frustrated working for a large and mature company like Flatliner, Inc. If you can offer challenge and opportunity to advance based on merit, I know I can offer the type of performance you expect of your top people.

May we discuss this further in person? I'll call you within a week to see if we can establish a mutual interest and to set an appointment at your convenience.

Thank you for your time and attention, and I certainly look forward to speaking with you soon.

Respectfully yours,

Samuel M. Vigil

Samuel M. Vigil

enclosure

JOYA CHANDRASKAR

931 Kentucky Street
Nashville, TN 37205

Telephone/Message:
(615) 555-0899

12 October 1994

*A recruiter told this candidate:
"This is the best cover letter I
have ever gotten in my life."*

David L. Grassi, M.D.
V.P., Sales
Wyon-LaRouche, Laboratory Division
317 Medical Plaza
Memphis, TN 37411

Dear Dr. Grassi:

I am still very interested in a pharmaceutical sales position with Wyon-LaRouche. Your response to my initial inquiry last year was quite encouraging, and I am following up as you requested. I have now received my B.A. from Tulane and am presently looking for a challenge I can sink my teeth into.

Of course, you will be interested in much more than my academic preparation. What you want to know is: Can this woman sell or what? You want to know if I can make things happen. Let me tell two stories that may shed some light on this question.

While working for a medical library affiliated with a hospital, I discovered that a bedside bookcart program had lapsed years ago. This program was designed to help inpatients gain access to primary and secondary medical literature pertaining to their illnesses. I researched the program's original design, developed a plan to integrate it into the library's extant operations, and went out and sold the program to the head librarian and to the doctors in the wards. Since my father is a doctor, I knew how to approach the doctors and present the benefits of allowing their patients to educate themselves. This is one example demonstrating my initiative, my ability to identify and persuade key decision-makers, and my ability to present those decision-makers with a ready-made solution. I learned long ago that presenting a comprehensive implementation plan results in action much more often than presenting a partial plan or just a raw idea.

Another recent example of my ability to recruit others into projects comes from my senior year at Tulane. As a midyear graduate, I wanted to have a midyear graduation ceremony, something Tulane did not deem worth the effort. I identified the key decision-maker in the administration and went and asked her what it would take to convince the university to hold a formal graduation ceremony. By enlisting her at such an early stage, I was able to learn exactly what it would take to motivate the rest of the administration. At her suggestion, I conducted two surveys, one to prove sufficient student interest, and a second to determine the format students wanted the ceremony to take, and what speakers students wanted to hear. I also recruited a corps of other midyear graduates to assist me and to collaborate with on the project. We presented the administration with a complete plan and budget for the graduation: ceremony, speakers, logistics, and various needed resources. This plan was implemented unchanged. The administration has decided to create a new tradition of midyear graduations, using this one as the model for all subsequent celebrations.

Dr. David Grassi
12 October 1994, page 2

I have many other stories like this. Even when I was in high school, I started a summer art school for children with a partner, and earned enough money for an international backpacking trip.

Finally, with my lifetime of interaction with medical professionals, and my diverse interests, ranging from classical music (ten years of formal study in violin) to Cajun dancing to photography to travel to sports to art, I am confident of my ability to succeed in building rapport with your target market. With my education and my technical aptitude, I am confident of my ability to represent your products.

Whether you are actively recruiting for sales positions at this time or not, please let us get together to discuss this further in person. I can be available for a meeting at your convenience. I will call you on Tuesday before noon to follow up on this mailing. You can count on me to be prompt, so if you will not be available on Tuesday morning, please advise your secretary as to a better time for me to reach you.

I appreciate your attention to this letter, and I certainly look forward to our conversation.

Sincerely,

Joya Chandraskar

Joya Chandraskar

Attachment: résumé

/jc

KENNETH L. HUFF

187 Middleton Lane
Danbury, Connecticut 06512

Telephone/Message:
(203) 555-4657

23 January 1995

Matthew M. Royston
Chief Market Analyst
Dunning Spongett Associates
47 Wall Street, Suite 201
New York, NY 10001

This candidate had a 100% response rate to this letter.

Dear Mr. Royston:

When you sell business consulting you have to sell confidence like a commodity. It's nice if your consulting is also valuable, but the critical act is selling the consulting in the first place. As an entrepreneur and a business consultant, I have proved my ability to identify and involve key players in my endeavors.

Whether my goal is to raise capital or sell my strategic consulting to principals of start-up businesses, I learned a long time ago that the relationship creates the sale. No fancy set of numbers makes anyone join me in a business venture. Either they have faith in me or they don't. The numbers simply back up that faith; they don't create it.

I think my greatest strength is that I can create that confidence and run the numbers, too. I can gain access to entrepreneurs and CEOs through my sales skills, and I can sustain that access because the quality of my consulting is, in fact, valuable.

When I told my business contacts that I was interested in becoming a broker, they told me, "Great. Let me know as soon as you have a position. I want you to review my portfolio." These are people I have worked with before. I may have fixed a business problem for them, leading to greater profits, or have led them to get involved in a project that paid back handsomely.

My special talent is accessing entrepreneurs just as they start to make it. There is a window of time after they start to have significantly positive cash flow and before they learn how to consume it in life-style changes, a time when they are very susceptible to guidance. Everybody knows that today's high-net-worth individuals are hounded by investment advisors, but tomorrow's high-net-worth individuals are not. They will respond best to somebody who speaks their own language. I know how to find these people before they show up in Dun & Bradstreet. Additionally, these are exciting people, comfortable with a high degree of change and stress, and they make excellent candidates for aggressive investment strategies.

Sure, I know how to grind out sales and marketing. I built a database of 50,000 customers (20,000 of them by personal introduction, 30,000 by advertising response). I'm not afraid of hard work—and I plan to work very hard—but I plan to work smart, too. Between my business contacts and my old school chums, I have a full book of clients already. I truly look forward to building a second and third tier of contacts.

I've been investigating this career option for almost a year. Let's discuss this further in person. I will call you on Thursday at exactly 10:30 A.M. Please advise your secretary to expect my call. If you are not available at that time, please have her suggest a better time to reach you.

Thank you.

Sincerely,

Kenneth L. Huff

Kenneth L. Huff

Paula Price

315 Oceanside Parkway
Malibu Beach, CA 90012
Telephone: (310) 555-8763

June 23, 1994

Mark Geiger
V.P., A&R
Big Brother Records
2931 Melrose Avenue, Suite 509
Los Angeles, CA 90005

Dear Mr. Geiger:

Once in a while someone wakes up and finds themselves living in the wrong life.

As a banker, I performed at 400% over quota for a two-year period, but no matter how many credits I earned toward my "superperson" plaque, I never felt like a banker.

As a personal banker, however, I struck up a friendship with John Lee Hooker. I attended the Grammys and the Bammies with him, and I was there when he and Carlos Santana began a jam session to develop a song for John's just-released album, *Mr. Lucky*. I have attended press interviews at his home and otherwise seen a little of the inside of the music business.

My current goal is to explore new career options that fit in better with my personality. I think anyone could see that I have gained some powerful sales and marketing skills (both organizational and interpersonal) as a banker. Now I want to transfer those skills into a new industry.

I am not one of those nice little ninnies who thinks she wants into the music business but doesn't want to do any work. On the contrary, I have had such success to date precisely because I love work. As a "for fun" project, I launched a nationwide licensed T-shirt sales/promotions company. So far, although we have made little money, I have proved that I can grind out the kind of contacts necessary to succeed in this business.

At this time, I am not applying for a position with you. I am just interested in having a conversation and discussing the business.

I think it's likely that one of your friends, or possibly someone in your own company, may be interested in someone with my unique background.

Let's talk more about this. I look forward to it. I'll ring you soon, so please keep this letter handy.

Yours sincerely,

Paula Price

PATRICIA J. O'KEEFE

3192 Balboa Avenue
San Francisco, California 94137
(415) 555-3827

June 17, 1994

This highly personal letter resulted in a call from a company that gets hundreds and sometimes thousands of letters every week.

Employment Department
Levi Strauss & Company
1155 Battery Street
San Francisco, California 94111

Dear Sir or Madam:

When I was sixteen, I became the proud owner of my first paycheck. My father suggested I frame the slip of paper, worth $20.86, as a keepsake. I had other plans. I went out and purchased a pair of Levi's 501 Buttonfly Jeans. Monopolizing the washer and dryer that afternoon running my new Levi's through three cycles, I waited impatiently, sitting upon the dryer. That pair of Levi's, which over the years have faded to white and frayed in areas, became a symbol of personal pride for me.

The enclosed résumé is also a symbol of personal pride. I chose to major in speech/communications to get a broad-based education that would allow me to develop the perceptiveness and skill to communicate effectively in business. My training in this field focused on a clear understanding of the role communications plays in our "mass mediated" society.

My work experience may at first glance look like I'm a waiter with an education. While that is true, it is not the whole truth. I take great care and pride in serving a quality product with style tailored to the needs of my guests. I am a professional in my work, always striving for a higher standard of excellence. I work efficiently under pressure of deadlines and quick changes of events. Waiting tables provided the time and income necessary to attend college full-time, as well as the security of knowing I possessed numerous skills useful in all business environments.

I believe in myself. New tasks become a challenge for me to be seen through to completion to the best of my abilities. I am an intelligent individual asking for an opportunity to begin with the best company in San Francisco. Once placed in a department, I will adapt and make it my own.

I would be proud to work for Levi Strauss and Co. I've yet to find anything cut to fit my style like a pair of Levi's 501 blues. Give someone who believes in quality an opportunity to grow with your company. Give me a call.

Sincerely,

Patricia J. O'Keefe

Patricia J. O'Keefe

Gordon Rocklin
3201 Woodstock Boulevard SE
Portland, Oregon 97202
(503) 555-2638

July 18, 1992

Mr. George Giardini
Bengal Motors N.A.
1501 Capon Avenue
Baltimore, Maryland 21227

Dear Mr. Giardini:

I am sending you this letter of introduction upon the suggestion of Mr. Paul Marten, your Seattle dealer and my friend. In my conversations with him, he has suggested that you and I may have something to talk about.

For most of my life I have been a motorcycle, bicycle, and car enthusiast and have been riding motorcycles since 1973. Since 1981 I have been a manufacturer's representative for Fujira bicycles, first setting up a dealer network in the New England states for a regional distributor of Fujira (Strivecycle), owned by Eugenia Rivetco. In 1984 I moved to Los Angeles and represented Fujira in the state of California, personally carrying on all functions of a regional office. I developed a fifty-dealer network selling well over a million dollars worth of bicycles annually. In 1987 I joined the main U.S. distributor, Fujira America, introducing Fujira to the Northwest while maintaining the California market. Presently I am responsible for approximately 100 dealers in the combined states of Alaska, Northern California, Idaho, Montana, Nevada, Oregon, and Washington. The challenge I have enjoyed while promoting Fujira has been to sell a higher-quality, but more expensive, product in a market that was traditionally price-conscious. Since 1990 I have been involved in the design, graphics, and color selection of many of the upper-end models. In this same period of time I have worked with the factory in Japan and with the dealers here in the U.S. to correct mechanical problems and have given both dealer sales training and mechanic orientation seminars. Making the understanding of mechanical fine points accessible to the dealer and the general public is enjoyable to me.

Over the years I have enjoyed a great deal of personal trust and freedom working for Fujira. I feel I have repaid that trust with hard work and perseverance, enabling Fujira to sell well in formerly less receptive markets. I have found this situation to be one in which I thrive and am able to work my best.

In the early years with Fujira, I was intensely interested in bicycling. During these years I also rode more than twenty thousand miles in the summers, servicing my accounts on a motorcycle—always a Bengal. As time has progressed, I have found that my interest has changed from bicycles to primarily motorcycles. I have become very involved in working with Bengals over the last three years. I am keenly interested in fine-tuning and improving Bengals for myself and for friends. (I have a LeMans III and an SX 1000 MS.) I have as much affection for these bikes in working on them as I have in riding them.

As a person involved in representing a manufacturer at the wholesale level and as a Bengal enthusiast, it is natural for me to contemplate Bengal Motors' future and determine if there is an opportunity to participate. The following, consequently, are my personal observations, based on conversations with owners and dealers, and my own thoughts.

George Giardini
July 18, 1992
page 2

The design simplicity of a Bengal illustrates a sophisticated approach to less is more. The bikes are practical, and yet unlike many other practical vehicles, have a very exciting and exotic quality to them. This, in my mind, separates the Bengal from its three strongest competitors (BMW, Cagiva, and Harley Davidson) for the more mature motorcycle dollar. I see the Bengal as having the most to offer the thirty- to fifty-year-old customer. However, I believe that success can only be achieved when you have a representative motivating dealers to carry and promote these bikes, teaching those dealers the proper techniques to sell the bikes, and creating and sustaining a successful image for Bengals. The bike can easily be promoted as combining the best traits of its three competitors in one product. It offers the exotic, handcrafted aura of a Cagiva/Ducati, the ease of maintenance, longevity, and respectability of a BMW, and the soulful earthy feel of a Harley Davidson. Yet most people inside and outside of motorcycling who talk to me when I am riding my Bengal are under the impression that Bengals are no longer manufactured or available! In the western states, Bengal Motors is well remembered by past owners but has otherwise almost completely dropped out of the public consciousness. As BMW and Harley Davidson have both improved their sales in the last few years and Cagiva has reentered the Ducati name into the marketplace, it seems there is a growing market share for the now middle-aged baby boomer, who is no longer feeling catered to by the big four Japanese manufacturers (who largely serve riders in their teens and twenties). I know that the lira's reevaluation has made the U.S. market difficult for the Bengal, as did the until-recent lack of California EQA certification.

Paul Marten mentioned to me that you may be considering opening a West Coast office. If there is any way I could be of help at present or in the future, either as a consultant or an employee, I would be interested in discussing this with you. My office number is 503-555-7796; my home number is 503-555-2638. Meanwhile, I have spoken to Paul about your next trip to the West Coast, and look forward to meeting you when you come.

Sincerely,

Gordon Rocklin

Gordon Rocklin

GR/dr

Chapter Six
Broadcast Letters for Headhunters

Headhunters Have Different Motivations

Headhunters are paid to find and deliver outstanding candidates who might otherwise be unavailable to the hiring company. They provide a valuabla niche service in the employment market, but they are not after just anybody. If you are a strong-performing, well-paid specialist who has been promoted several times over the last few years, and have a bright future in a burgeoning industry, headhunters are very likely to appear in your employment future. If you are an unemployed generalist, recently over- or underpaid, with a zigzagging career path, or are currently attempting to engineer a career transition, headhunters are very unlikely to be interested in you *even if you could excel in the position they are searching to fill.*

Although it is a good idea to contact headhunters periodically, especially while you are employed and things are going well, no one should base a job search on headhunters. That's because of the way headhunters work: they find people for jobs, not jobs for people. Even if a headhunter just happens to think you are wonderful, she can't do anything for you unless by some fluke you are exactly the type of person she has a job order for at that moment.

Consequently, you need to contact a large number of headhunters to get any benefit from contacting them at all. In the ideal job search—you are employed and have a solid, rapidly progressing career path—you should send a letter to every single headhunter who specializes in your particular field. This can be hundreds, possibly even a few thousand.

To learn more about headhunters and how they work, read *The Headhunter Strategy* by Ken Cole and *Rights of Passage at $100,000+* by John Lucht.

To learn about more headhunters, buy a custom printout from The Recruiting & Search Report (a publishing company, 904-235-3733 or 800-634-4548), or look in *The Directory of Executive Recruiters* available from Kennedy Publications (603-585-2200 or 603-585-6544).

What Headhunters Are Looking For

Many candidates spend a great deal of time crafting letters to headhunters in hopes of winning some kind of special consideration. They start out saying "I got your name from a friend in the industry" and go on to reiterate the high points of their résumés.

Some of the headhunters I've talked to say they *never* read unsolicited letters. Others hire a ten-dollar-an-hour clerk to feed unsolicited résumés into a database and filing system. Others say they can sort a foot-high stack of mail in as little as ten or fifteen minutes, by skipping the letters altogether and just glancing over the résumés.

What's my point? Don't spend a lot of time and effort on your letters to headhunters. If they have an active search on for someone exactly like you, they'll give you a call. If you know, or can get an introduction to, one in your industry, send him a résumé and hound him for a little advice. That's all.

Here is a radical piece of advice: Once you have prepared a target list of headhunters using one of the two resources cited above, prepare a generic "Dear Placement Specialist:" letter and just photocopy the darn thing. You'll save a bundle on word-processing, and the impact will be virtually the same.

What do headhunters skim for?

directly related experience

appropriate educational credentials

current employment status

Of course there will be exceptions, but in general you must be currently employed in a position directly related to their current search efforts, with a full set of educational credentials, to catch a headhunter's eye. Keep your letter short, as they are not likely to read much of it, anyway. If you have a precise target, make a "routing slip" notation at the top of your letter, such as:

Attn: Recruiter - Hospitality Specialist

Re: General Manager - Resort Properties

Also see the routing slip section in chapter 3, "Cover Letters for Announced Openings" (pp. XX). A related technique is to state your interest in the very first line of your letter, possibly in bold: "If you have any clients who may be in need of a **corporate communications manager with multimedia expertise** then perhaps we could be of use to one another."

Let Headhunters Know that You Understand Their Business

Use language that shows you understand how headhunters work. For instance, while you would never ask a headhunter to find or offer you a job, you could ask for an "introduction to one of your clients." Be specific: "I should think that an introduction to one of your clients who may need a little assistance with remote-sensing technology could be of benefit to all concerned."

Know that headhunters also worry that you may embarrass them if they present you to a client, that you could come off as a know-nothing dud. So you might mention that you can "make a compelling presentation of my candidacy whether I am actually selected for a position or not."

It is okay to let headhunters know your salary range, especially if you are sure of it. "I currently earn in the high 80s (salary + bonus), and would expect to break into six figures to make a move." Of course, you need not reveal anything concerning salary outside of a personal meeting. See chapter 9, "Salary Histories."

Although it is certainly not an issue you need to address in a preliminary letter, headhunters will be interested in your reason for wanting to leave a company. An impending layoff, a personality dispute, a "difference of opinion concerning the future direction of the company," and similar situations are probably best kept to yourself. However, saying that you are stymied by lack of room to exercise your ambition will definitely interest them. Here are some examples:

> Because of my rank as Chief Financial Officer for a family-owned business, it is almost impossible for me to advance further in my present company.

❖

> This company is quite healthy, but despite record sales and profitability, there are few challenges on the horizon for the next few years. Of course, I could draw a fine salary while serving secure accounts, but I am motivated to seek greater challenges.

❖

> I am perfectly comfortable where I am, but I am generating ideas and projects much faster than can be utilized by my current employer. My proposals are accepted enthusiastically, but project rollout rate is nearly glacial. I have come to realize that I might be happier in an arena that is more dynamic.

As a related point, warning headhunters of your need for confidentiality will give them the impression that you are likely to be secure and well respected in your current position. Here is an example:

> If you find my background of interest, I would like to meet with your client as soon as is feasible. As my current employer is quite happy with me and my future here seems bright, I need your utmost confidentiality.

The One Clause Every Letter to a Headhunter Should Contain

Although it is against industry ethics, headhunters can float your candidacy to prospective employers without notifying you of this act. This is not necessarily to your advantage. You want the headhunter to advance you for opportunities you could never have discovered on your own, not float your résumé to employers you already planned to contact. Remember, the headhunter expects to collect her placement fee if you are hired by any company she contacts about you. So it's a good idea to include some version of the following clause in your first mailing to any headhunter:

> Of course it is understood that you would not advance my materials to any employer without discussing the specific opportunity with me first.

Go for It

Take a look at the following examples, and good luck!

RICHARD CHASE

Consulting Engineer / Engineering Manager

1932 Cuyahoga Street, Suite 132
Cincinnati, Ohio 45802-7213

Office: (513) 555-3982
Residence: (513) 555-1192

Date: 3 November 1994
Attn: Senior Consultants, Specialists in Engineering & Technology
Re: Project Manager—Agricultural Engineering / Mechanical Engineering

Dear Placement Specialist:

Do you have any clients who have engineering projects that are behind schedule? Do your clients have any smaller projects which they wish they could pursue, but just don't have the time or the staff?

If you have a client who would like to bring a development or a production effort back on track, or if you have a client who would like to pursue a project outside of internal channels, then here's what I have to offer: a track record of success in projects ranging from mechanical equipment to agricultural equipment to consumer products (see résumé). My strengths are new-product development, prototyping, and problem solving.

I can troubleshoot the project as an external consultant, manage the project out-of-house, or come inside and work directly with your client's engineering team. I can also season younger engineers who may be great at technical matters but need a little guidance to keep a project on track. Also, I can assist you in planning, feasibility analysis, customer relations, and other issues.

As a hands-on manager with a strong technical background, there are many ways I could be of use to one of your clients. Of course I'd want to discuss particular situations before you forward my résumé to anyone. Perhaps the best thing for us to do would be to have a brief "get acquainted" chat to see if we have a mutual interest. I am available at one of the above telephone numbers.

Thank you for your consideration, and I look forward to our conversation.

Sincerely,

Richard Chase

Richard Chase

Enclosure

Susan Sturgis

521 Oceanside Avenue, Apt. 2
Brooklyn, New York 11723

Telephone/Message:
(718) 555-3906

December 1, 1995

Attn: Tim McNulty
Sales Consultants
10 Washington Place
New York, New York 10031

Dear Tim:

Thank you for your time on the phone last week.

As you will note from my résumé, I have ten years of broadcast sales and advertising planning experience. I would like to make a change sometime in the coming year.

I think I have a lot to offer, given my consistent sales achievements and my knowledge of strategic positioning and the "bigger picture."

My greatest interest at this point is exploratory—learning more about your needs and the types of positions you fill. Hopefully we will be able to establish a mutual interest.

I would like to reserve some time to meet with you. I will give you a call to see if we can get together. Of course it is understood that you would not forward my materials to a potential employer without discussing the specific opportunity with me first.

Yours sincerely,

Susan Sturgis

Susan Sturgis

Enclosure

MAUREEN KILLIAN O'DALY

140 West 74th, 12th Front
New York, New York 10028

Private Telephone/Voicemail: (212) 555-1843
Private Fax: (212) 555-3662

August 20, 1994

Attn: Steven M. Bridger
Principal
Thorn, Bridger Associates, Inc.
11 E. 44th St.
New York, NY 10017

Dear Mr. Bridger:

I'm sure that from time to time you run across a candidate who defies easy classification. With a diversified career in **marketing**, **publishing**, **advertising,** and conception/promotion of major **events**, I think I may fit that description.

A quick glance at my résumé and references will reveal that my greatest asset is my ability to bring people together to their mutual benefit. (This is not unlike what you do, of course.)

Working in the new and rapidly expanding field of **integrated marketing**, I have put together several highly successful and innovative joint promotions involving, for example, Range Rover, Neiman Marcus, Ritz-Carlton Hotels, ABC Sports, the Hong Kong Tourism Board, Baccarat, Moet et Chandon, Julia Child, BMW, and so on, virtually ad infinitum. I have direct connections worldwide with top people in the tourism, wine, food, fashion, and media industries. More to the point, I have proven that I can make connections easily in any area where I may need them.

In more traditional strategic management areas, I took a local Hawaiian resort magazine and made it a worldwide mouthpiece that promoted Hawaii's resorts on an even level with the best in Europe and, indeed, worldwide. I built an entrepreneurial management team that launched one of the most successful high-end publications in recent years, Life & Leisure magazine, a significant promotional vehicle whose readership has an average household income of $95,000+. In short, I bring a track record of success in media and marketing projects, including solid financial, staffing, and operations-management skills.

I expect that I might be able to establish a mutual interest with one of your clients in marketing, media, advertising, public relations, and/or promotions. Given my high-profile involvement with my current company, I'm sure you understand my need for a discrete introduction and, of course, it is understood that you would not advance my candidacy to any employer without discussing the particular opportunity with me first.

If you do have any clients who could benefit from an innovator and deal-maker with my skills, then I am sure we could have an interesting meeting whether we arrange a placement or not.

Thank you for your consideration. I look forward to your call.

Sincerely,

Maureen Killian O'Daly

MKD/dw

KENNETH E. TAKAHARA

17 Wildflower Way   Office: (303) 555-6612
Golden, Colorado 80913   Residence: (303) 555-4742

March 19, 1995

Placement Specialist
90 S. Cascade Avenue, Suite 5155, B-21
Denver, Colorado 81022

Dear Placement Specialist:

I was very interested to read your advertisement in last week's *Wall Street Journal* for a V.P. of Project Services for an alternative energy company. I have enclosed my résumé for your review. I think you may find my background pertinent.

After six years of experience in natural resources, I went into the world of utilities finance. I currently rank in my company's top quintile of revenue producers, where I consult with sophisticated investors on a full spectrum of utilities investments. This experience has sharpened my communication, analytical, and public relations skills, as I deal daily with top executives and other prominent individuals from coast to coast. My current goal is to utilize these financial and communication skills in a position such as the one you advertised, contributing to an energy/natural resources company. In addition, I suspect some of my current contacts would be of benefit in such a position.

Since my office is not far from yours, I'd appreciate a brief meeting to discuss this personally. I am confident that I could make a compelling presentation of my candidacy to your client and would welcome the opportunity to do so.

Sincerely,

Kenneth E. Takahara

Kenneth E. Takahara

Enclosure

Chapter Seven
Thank-You Letters

Timeliness Is Next to Godliness

When a thank-you letter arrives is more important than what it says. You should write and post thank-yous *the same day* as the meeting or the phone call referenced. A simple note such as the following is sufficient:

Dear Ms. Orr:

Thank you for your time today. I was impressed by Orr Industries, and I hope a tax analyst position opens up soon. I'll be calling you once every ten days, as you suggested. Also, thanks so much for the referral to Jason T. Colson. We have an appointment already.

Again, thank you, and I'll be in touch.

Sincerely,

Your Name Here

Here is a more expansive model:

Dear Mr. Thompson:

Thank you for the introduction to your office in our meeting of January 28. I am drawn to the professionalism and dedication that you and Ms. Whitney exhibited, and I look forward to learning more about your operations in our next meeting.

I am confident of my skills and abilities as related to the position, and I hope I was able to convey those skills to you. I would particularly like to point out to you my extensive experience in a financial environment.

The sum of my education and my experience, I believe, provides a solid base for the demands of this position. I look forward to our next meeting this Thursday, at which time I will be happy to answer any additional questions you may have.

Respectfully yours,

Your Name Here

Send a thank-you letter to the interviewer and anyone else who met with you for more than just a moment. If you meet with seven people, send a thank-you letter to each and every one of them. The letters can be virtually identical, but should be individually addressed. *Be careful about names and titles*. During the interview sessions, collect the business cards of everyone you meet, or make a point of asking for this information before you leave. If you have to, call back and ask a receptionist to give you the correct spelling of everybody's name and their exact titles.

Although a thank-you letter should be sent right away, it's still better send it a week to ten days late than not at all. If you've waited any longer than that, turn to chapter 11, "Continuing Interest Letters," and model your letter after the ones you see there.

Longer thank-you letters can be typed on standard 8½ × 11 stationery. Certain shorter letters can be hand-printed on monarch (7¼ × 10½) or note-size (5½ × 8½) stationery or, if they are quite short, typed on conservative, understated greeting cards (which you can buy at any drugstore or stationers). Do not hand-write any letters unless you are an informal person applying for an informal position with an informal employer. When in doubt, type your letters.

Praise Your Recipient

A good thank-you letter goes beyond gratitude for the meeting and actually praises the recipient, her department, her colleagues, her company, her industry, and her golf handicap. Yes, if you sound like a saccharine sycophant or a cloying toady your letter might be viewed as insincere, but if you honestly try you can always find plenty to praise. Note how both of the two letters above open with a dose of praise, as does this example:

> I really enjoyed our meeting earlier this week. You were quite informative about the firm and the strong opportunities there. It is always a pleasure to speak with someone who loves what they do.

Using the Thank-You Letter to Further Your Case

In addition to the sort of polite thank-you letters discussed above, there are thank-you letters that can bolster your candidacy, provide additional evidence against any shortcomings that the employer may have brought up in the interview, and remedy what the French call esprit d'escalier, or the wit of the staircase, those clever remarks you wish you had said at the party, but which did not occur to you until you were on your way down to the street.

Here is an example of how to use a thank-you letter to overcome an interview shortcoming:

> Marty, in our meeting you asked me the question, "Why venture capital?" It occurred to me later that I may have failed to answer that question with the depth of thinking that I have given the issue. It is no accident that I decided to contact you—I have been considering this career move for some time. After my stints as a Big 6 department manager and as CFO of an entrepreneurial company, I am personally and professionally ready for it. As we discussed, it is precisely the project-oriented nature of the work that attracts me the most. I am seeking an environment that will provide consistent challenges for my combination of financial, marketing, and management strengths. I think Wilson Saperstein has that kind of environment.

By the way, never leave an interview without finding out what happens next: how many interviews will there be, when the next cycle of interviews begins, when they plan to have a decision by, and the approximate date they hope to have the new hire start. Memorize this sentence: "Mike, I know you'll be getting back to me. At what point—if I don't hear from you—should I be back in touch with you?"

Go for It

Take a look at the following examples, and good luck!

BRENDA J. HYDE

1622 - 25th Street, #1
Richmond, California 94801

Office/Voicemail: (510) 555-0455
Residence/Message: (510) 555-0335

December 1, 1994

Martin Harnwold
Director, U.S. Pacemaker Sales
Trimedics, Inc.
14000 Technology Drive
Angleton, Texas 77515

Dear Mr. Harnwold:

Thank you for the wonderful experience of meeting with you and your associates last week. I hope this is just the beginning of a long and mutually beneficial relationship.

The day after Thanksgiving I called one of my cardiologist friends, Dr. Mark Nalgren, to discuss your company. In addition to saying wonderful things about your products, he invited me to observe a case that day. The patient had a lead adapter that had blown a Palmsign pacemaker, and Dr. Nalgren opted to replace the Palmsign with an Trimedics implant. He presented the case to me, and by the end of the case I knew this was a product I could back 100%.

I think it is particularly telling that John and Bill got my name from my own customers. They know me best. They know I keep my word, and they know I know my product lines (and my competitors') to the last technical detail. They trust me, and that translates into access and sales.

You and your team excited me about Trimedics. Your requirements fit my skills and background well, your enthusiasm for my candidacy was certainly appreciated, and I think we have a good potential for a fit. I've already begun training myself on the medical issues surrounding your products.

As we discussed, I'm forwarding employer and customer references. I hope this fulfills your needs, but if you should want any additional data, you can count on me for a prompt response.

I'll ring you within 24 hours of your receipt of this letter to follow up. Thank you for your time. I appreciate the consideration.

Yours sincerely,

Brenda J. Hyde

enclosure
cc: John Darling, Bill Bankman

```
Barbara Weyer
6335 Melville Drive
Sherman Oaks, California 91403


January 31, 1995


John Paoulos, District Marketing Manager
Kaiser Foundation Health Plans
2910 Geary Boulevard
San Francisco, California 94115


Dear John:

Thank you for another enjoyable meeting.  I remain ever more convinced
of the potential for a good match here and hope that your review of my
portfolio will convince you of the same.

John, you mentioned that you saw this position as a transition for me,
from the provider side to the community outreach side.  Actually, the
bulk of my background is more directly related to this job than my
most recent experience indicates.  Again, my portfolio makes a strong
statement about my skills in this area.  Finally, my references will
attest to my potential to deliver on your behalf.

If there is any aspect of my background that you would like further
elucidated, please don't hesitate to give me a ring.  I will call you
next week if I have not heard from you by then.  I look forward to our
next conversation, and I appreciate your attention to the materials I
have submitted.

By the way, everyone in my professional network has been very
encouraging about Kaiser as an employer.  Nothing could make me
happier than to join the Kaiser "community."

Yours sincerely,


Barbara Weyer


Barbara Weyer

Enclosure
/bw
```

Carlton Werner

2323 Gibson Street
Hoboken, New Jersey 07120
(201) 555-7104

August 25, 1995

Attn: Stuart A. Miller
Andrew Harmon & Company
317 Vesey Street
New York, NY 10001

Dear Mr. Miller:

I have been away on an unexpected trip to Europe, and I wanted to get back to you right away. I really enjoyed our meeting earlier this month, and I appreciate your introduction to Mr. Hui. The meeting made a strong impression on me, and I appreciate your time and consideration.

After significant thought I have decided that the challenge and the opportunity available within Andrew Harmon's financial appraisal and marketing group is very appealing indeed. I would like to explore further the possibility of specializing in financial appraisal of companies.

My strong financial analysis skills and successful M&A experience should allow me to master the principles of valuation very quickly. My combination of analytical and interpersonal skills would be of direct application as both a marketing representative and a service provider.

I would like to take you up on your offer to introduce me to some of the partners in your office. I'll be calling you soon to arrange a convenient date and time.

Again, I appreciate your time and consideration. I look forward to speaking with you soon.

Sincerely,

Carlton Werner
CW/yw

Susan Guerrero
51 Capra Way
San Francisco, CA 94123
(415) 555-7249

The Crevasse, Inc.
One Harrison Street
San Francisco, CA 94105
(415) 555-2905

Attn: Tierney Britz, Executive Recruiter

June 27, 1994

Dear Tierney:

Thank you for your time yesterday and for your confidence in my potential. I am very excited by The Crevasse as a company, and I am sure that I could make a meaningful contribution when the time is right for both of us.

Although my technical/analytical skills have been a solid entrée into the business, I think my long-term potential is better defined by my enthusiasm for all aspects of the apparel business. I believe a mix of analyst and aesthetician is required—part scientist and part artist—for continuing success.

I will certainly be in regular contact with you in the coming months, keeping you updated on what is going on with me, and also keeping a finger on the pulse at The Crevasse.

Thanks again for your time, and I look forward to our next conversation.

Yours sincerely,

Susan Guerrero

Susan Guerrero

Chapter Eight
Reference Sheets

Select a Pool of References

Early in your job search you should decide whom you are going to use for references. The best choices are superiors who worked relatively closely with you. Work peers are okay in a pinch, but subordinates are definitely not going to impress anyone. Your priest, rabbi, club associates, and other people who know you socially are unacceptable.

A reference need not have a fancy title; they just need to know your work. A company officer who thinks you are wonderful but has no direct on-the-job experience with you is not as strong a reference as you might think. Some candidates use former coworkers who have left the company, vendors, or customers as references, especially when trying to run a clandestine job search.

In this day and age when most companies have strict policies about giving references, potential employers no longer expect every reference to be forthcoming and loquacious. However, references who refer the caller to human resources or say, "It is our policy only to confirm or not confirm the former employee's title, dates of employment, and approximate ending salary," are definitely not going to make any points for you with a potential employer. And if *all* your contacts seem afraid to talk about you, potential employers will assume there is a big problem.

Reprinted by permission of Tribune Media Service

Don't worry if you can't generate a reference for each and every job on your résumé. Companies do go out of business, divisions are eliminated, stuff happens. It is a good business practice, however, to try and stay in touch with at least one person from every place you have worked over the last ten to fifteen years.

You need to ask permission to use someone as a reference, and it's a good idea to forward them a copy of your latest résumé. (See chapter 4, "Networking Letters.") Go ahead and prep them by telling them what they ought to remember about you: "If someone calls, Mike, be sure to mention that I opened the EEC for the company and that I negotiated the largest order in company history to that date. I'd sure appreciate it." By the way, if you are afraid to send your résumé to your references, it's a pretty strong sign that there's inflated information on your résumé that should be rewritten.

Your pool of references should include seven to ten individuals so that you can rotate your references so that no one reference gets a series of calls about you. After all, the last thing you want is for a reference to become annoyed with excess calls and mouth off something like, "Jeez, hasn't he gotten a job yet?" This actually happened when I called a reference given by somebody applying for a job with my company. Needless to say, I did not hire that individual.

At the risk of belaboring the obvious, I repeat: each reference should be somebody who had direct working knowledge of you and would be willing to say wonderful things about your skills, judgment, work habits, likability, productivity, and business savvy.

If anyone is reluctant to be a reference for you, *do not mention them.* If you have any reason to doubt what any of your references might say, it is not unreasonable to have a very smooth friend call them, perhaps pretending to be a headhunter, and check it out.

Selection and Presentation

Unless told otherwise, prepare three to five references. Tailor your references to the particular application. For example, if a potential employer seems concerned about your financial skills, your first reference should be someone who can describe a financial problem you solved, or a financial project you managed.

A reference listing provides the contact's name, current title and business address, and current daytime telephone number. Be careful not to give out anyone's home telephone number without explicit permission. If your connection to any reference is not obvious, state it in parentheses. Be sure not to list only men or only women. Here's an example of how to format:

References:
  Bill Clinton
  President, United States
  (formerly Governor, Arkansas, when I was Chief of the Arkansas State Police)
  The White House
  Washington, D.C. 20500
  (202) 456-1111

Go for It

Take a look at the following example, and good luck!

BARTO JONES

17 East 45th Street, Penthouse
New York, New York 10017

Office/Voicemail: (212) 555-0495
Residence/Message: (212) 555-0345

REFERENCES:

Robert I. Bernstein, Ph.D., President
Cramer & Gould, Inc.
551 Madison Avenue
New York, New York 10022
800-526-4243 (please see attached letter)

Simon Sturgeon, C.P.A., Manager, International Accounting
(formerly CFO of Cramer & Gould, Inc.)
Murdoch & Murdoch Worldwide Manufacturing Representation, Inc.
521 Fifth Avenue
New York, New York 10175
800-555-3158
212-555-1003

Thomas G. Billotson, V.P. Human Resources
Baxter Financial Services Corp.
One Park Plaza
New York, New York 10010
212-555-3501
212-555-3869

Shelly Perry, V.P. Operations
Daig & Associates, Inc.
25 West 43rd Street, Suite 812
New York, New York 10036
212-555-2793

Chapter Nine
Salary Histories

When to Provide Salary Data

The first thing you have to understand about salary data is that it is always exclusionary. That means that it will be used only to eliminate you from consideration—unless you are grossly underpaid now and applying to an employer who is eager to continue paying you well below the market rate. If you are earning too much, the prospective employer will imagine that you would be unhappy in the position she has to fill. If you make too little, on the other hand, she will undervalue your claimed experience and skills. If you used to make more than you do now, she will think your career has floundered. And if you make considerably more now than you did quite recently, she will consider you an uncertain quantity, perhaps only a flash in the pan.

Even a salary background that's exactly what an employer has in mind still doesn't qualify you for the position; it just qualifies you for further consideration. Since there are so many ways this data can count against you, and virtually no way to count for you, you should almost never mention salary in a first mailing. In rare cases, an employer will arbitrarily ignore candidates who do not comply with a request for salary data, but this is not as common as employers using salary data to eliminate a majority of candidates. If your application is strong and you can convince the employer of your ability to excel in the position, you need not provide salary data before a first interview.

You can ignore a request for salary data entirely, or acknowledge it with one of these lines at the very bottom of your letter:

> Salary data provided on interview.

> Salary: Negotiable.

The following is the best oblique response to a salary inquiry that I have ever read:

> My salary has been within industry norms for each position, and I assume that you can afford to offer a competitive salary, as well as challenge and opportunity.

Providing salary data is *not* the same thing as negotiating a salary and perks. In general, you should avoid providing salary data before an interview, then let them bring up the topic first. Respond to any questions about *your* salary with a question about *their* salary ("What range did you have in mind for this position?"). Always negotiate salaries in person, never over the phone, and whenever possible delay such negotiations until they have made you a solid job offer. For more on negotiating salary, see my *Overnight Job Change Strategy* or Jack Chapman's *How to Make $1000 a Minute*. Also see chapter 6, "Broadcast Letters for Headhunters," for how to provide salary history or requirements to a headhunter in a *preliminary* mailing.

How Accurate Should You Be?

Determining how much money you make now is not as simple as you might at first think. If you consider your total compensation package as a mixture of cash and perks, you can report your salary history with considerable flexibility. Between after-tax "take-home pay" and "total compensation package" is a huge grey area you can call your remuneration. **Never misrepresent your salary, but never miss the best way to represent your salary.**

Focusing on taxable income can deflate your salary figure; focusing on your total package can inflate it. Some candidates do both, presenting a range that, while they can explain it honestly, seems vague and mysterious enough that an employer can't use it to exclude them from consideration:

> Salary and compensation fell in the range of $43,000 to $68,800, depending on how you value my particular compensation package.

(See the computation table about how to come up with these ranges.)

Some candidates use rounded figures and open-ended statements to obscure salary data:

> Base salary was in the mid 30s, plus a liberal package—bonus, allowance, and overrides—amounting to considerably more.

You can use the same kind of smoke screen in response to questions about salary requirements. First of all, do not use the word "requirements" when discussing your salary "objectives." "Requirements" is a rigid word, and is not conducive to fluid negotiating. Here is an example:

> My salary objectives would be in the range from the high sixties to near six figures, depending on the particular arrangement of cash and perks which we are able to agree on. I am quite interested in this opportunity, and am sure we will be able to come to terms when we get to the stage where we have to work out such details.

HOW TO TURN $43,000 INTO $68,800

Your base pay:	$43,000,
Plus your estimated bonus:	4,000,
Plus your next raise, if imminent:	4,300,
Plus the value of your perks:	
Company auto that you drive 25,000 miles per year:	13,000,
Matching contribution to company-sponsored retirement plan:	2,000,
Life and health insurance:	1,900,
Average four sick days each year your company lets you cash out:	600,
Your compensation package:	**$68,800,**

Salary Tables

Provide your salary history on a separate sheet of paper, with the same heading as your cover letter and/or your résumé (name, address, phone number). No matter what an employer requests, you have the option of providing less. For example, some candidates routinely give information only on their last job or the last ten years.

Salary tables traditionally give each employer's name, followed by your title, dates of employment, and ending salary, as in this example:

Bovine Weightloss Clinics, Inc., Dallas, Texas, 1991-1993
Assistant Controller
Salary: $42,500 plus incentives and bonus

Go for It

Take a look at the following example, but remember that you don't need to provide this much information if you think it might count against you. Good luck!

Russell Jackson

6750 La Cienega Boulevard
Los Angeles, California 90056
Residence: (213) 555-9044
24-hour message: (213) 555-0199

SALARY HISTORY

CRUISE TIME, Miami, Florida, 1993-Present
Sales Manager
Compensation: $85,000 base plus bonus and overrides amounting to considerably more.

HOST SYSTEMS, Miami, Florida, 1990-1993
Team Leader
Compensation: $57,000 base plus bonus, car, and travel allowance.

INCENTIVE SOLUTIONS, INC., Dallas, Texas, 1987-1990
Sales Manager
Compensation: $61,000 base plus bonus and car.

LEISURE SHARES, Honolulu, Hawaii, 1984-1987
Sales Counselor
Compensation: over $100,000 in top year.

Chapter Ten
Letters of Recommendation

When to Include Letters of Recommendation

In recent years a sort of grade inflation has hit letters of recommendation. A perfectly good letter from a decade or so ago now seems ho-hum. Today, these letters tend to be so laudatory that unless yours say you can walk on water, you're probably better off *not* including them with your initial cover letter and résumé.

However, if you *do* have a short, concise letter that says you can walk on water, consider including a copy with every mailing you send out. Any letter of recommendation sent in a preliminary mailing needs to be industry-related—a sales manager will not care at all what a high-school principal has to say about your tremendous success in the teaching field, and vice versa. Slip letters that you decide not to mail into your briefcase and take them to any interview or meeting. Incidentally, always ask for letters of recommendation whenever leaving an employer. They can really boost your job search, and they're usually an ego booster as well.

If You Have to Write Your Own

In the event that you ask for a letter of recommendation and the boss says, "You write it; I'll sign it," you have a golden opportunity. *Do not hold back.* This is not the time to be shy or humble. Take advantage of the golden opportunity to present yourself as a singularly outstanding employee. Write it as though you really were your boss. Remember, if he doesn't like something you have written, he can always ask you to change it.

In an effective letter of recommendation, the author first **demonstrates his credentials** for writing such a letter. What was the writer's position relative to the employee? How long did the writer have direct contact with the employee? How closely did the writer supervise/observe her?

Next, just as in an oral job reference, the writer should address the employee's **job responsibilities, skills, judgment, work habits, likability, productivity,** and **business savvy.** She may tell one or more stories about the employee's particular projects or triumphs. To remain believable and demonstrate objectivity, some letters contain a modicum of criticism or warn of some weakness. In a *really* good letter, the weakness is chosen to be attractive to the potential employer: "If Johanna has any fault it is that she spends too much time working late at the office when it's not really necessary, but since she always seems to be in a good mood, I guess there's no harm in that." Bold letter writers will rank the employee relative to all other employees that have ever held similar positions: "Brad is the best buyer we've ever had," or "Brad certainly ranks in the top 5% of retail managers I've ever had the pleasure to work with."

Finally, the letter may predict the wonderful career development this employee is capable of: "Johanna has the potential to make an excellent national sales manager some day." My favorite sentence like this is: "I recommend Johanna without reservation for any position for which she may be qualified." That's a fail-safe recommendation, wouldn't you say? Another good one is, "We're sorry to lose Johanna, but our loss is your gain. If you can offer her the challenge and the opportunity she deserves, she will make an outstanding employee."

In these litigious days, most letters do not say, "We'd hire Brad back in a minute if we could," as some "Brads" have taken such words a little too literally.

Most letters close with a line like this: "Should you need to hear any more wonderful things about Brad, please feel free to give me a call at 213-555-8218."

Go for It

Take a look at the following examples, and good luck!

November 21, 1994

TO WHOM IT MAY CONCERN:

Tanya Fox served our company during summers and holidays over a six-year period, 1988-1994. During this time she practically became part of our family. Tanya started out as a seasonal sales associate, but we soon found out she was anything but just another seasonal employee.

In six years, we never found anything Tanya could not do. She was consistently able to do the work of two employees, and we have many very good employees in our four locations.

Tanya's warmth, enthusiasm, and good spirit would endear her to anybody, but as an employer we grew to appreciate her integrity and work ethic even more. Tanya always identified with our management interests, and she could be trusted explicitly. Some of her duties included opening, closing, merchandising, stock and inventory, markups/markdowns, sales analysis, and balancing daily receipts. Where Tanya shines, however, is in dealing with customers and coworkers. We soon learned to put new workers with Tanya to get them started on the right track.

Tanya also seemed to have a fine understanding of our customer base, and I came to appreciate her judgment on trends and product mix. When she accompanied me on a buying trip to New York, she was a consummate professional. Her selections were consistently winners.

I recommend Tanya Fox without reservation. She has what it takes to excel in any business. Should you need any additional information, please feel free to call me directly.

Sincerely,

Jeremy Butler

Jeremy Butler

Owner/Manager

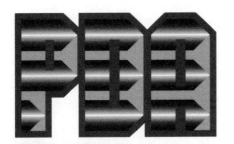

PDA Associates Ltd.
Advertising
56 Wellington Road Ballsbridge Dublin 2 Ireland
Tel 559269 Fax 551431

IN PRAISE OF JOHN McGLEENAN

It is customary in a public reference such as this to speak kindly and well of the person to whom it refers.

It is more difficult however to communicate clearly the degree of absolute confidence with which I can recommend John as an Audio-Visual Producer.

John's role in PDA Associates involved the routine, the technical, and the creative. He cast, produced, and directed radio commercials for many of the agency's leading clients; in particular, commercials that I had written. More recently, he undertook the role of TV producer with equal facility. His technical skills were regularly put to the test in co-ordinating multimedia presentations both in the agency and outside.

John leaves PDA Associates having learned a lot and contributed a lot. He has, in effect, "outgrown" the challenges we have to offer.

If you have similar or, preferably, greater challenges, I know John will respond co-operatively and with great skill, enthusiasm, and team spirit.

I wish John well, knowing he deserves to do well, and will do well.

BRENDAN O'BROIN
Creative Director
20th August 1994

SOUTHERN BEHAVIOR HEALTH, INC.

11938 ATLANTIC EXPRESSWAY • CAPE CANAVERAL, FL 32920 • (407) 555-HELP

Tabatha Stevens
Clinical Supervisor

August 18, 1994

TO WHOM IT MAY CONCERN:

As Case Management Team Leader, I have had clinical oversight of Drew McCormick for the last two and one-half years here at Southern Behavioral Health (SBH).

She was Intake Team Leader for the first two years, handling triage, emergencies, referrals, and administration of hospitalizations. Although the position Drew held was originally structured as an intake function, she did in fact take on a clinical role almost immediately. Subject to review by credentialed personnel, she prepared preliminary treatment plans and provided significant crisis intervention by telephone. Patient diagnoses included a wide range of dysfunction, from anxiety disorders to acute psychoses.

Since the beginning of this year, she has been involved in a special project to plan and implement an aftercare program. Under the tutelage of the Director of Intake, she designed, implemented, and documented the new program and trained others to run it. In this role she has been in charge of the training and orientation of five Aftercare Specialists.

Drew is an outstanding employee—dedicated, zealous, and careful. Her clinical skills are exceptional, and she is clearly going to be one of those rare psychotherapists who brings a fine intuitive sense as well as a fine analytical mind. She is good-natured and highly productive, and is well liked by her coworkers and colleagues.

Ms. McCormick easily ranks in the top 1% of clinical professionals that I have ever had the pleasure to know. In short, I recommend Drew without reservation for any position for which she may be qualified. Should you need any additional or more specific information, please feel free to call me directly.

Sincerely,

Tabatha Stevens, Ph.D.

Tabatha Stevens, Ph.D.

cc: File

Chapter Eleven
Continuing Interest Letters

Why Send One?

A hiring authority may meet with ten people in a day, or he may meet with a few dozen people over the course of a month. Sometimes a simple hiring program can take many, many weeks, as key executives fly in and out of town, the search criteria change in midproject, and/or the first-, second-, and third-choice candidates all decline the offer. Even a promising candidate can get lost in this shuffle.

A lead on a job opening should be considered "closed" only when someone is hired for the position *and* it looks like he is going to work out. Otherwise, the lead is still active and you have as good a shot at the position as anyone else. Unless an employer tells you unequivocally that the position has gone to another candidate, stay very interested.

As time drags on, even an employer who was initially excited about your qualifications may forget all about you. Hiring projects can be messy, inefficient, and prolonged, just like a job search. You can help yourself stay in the running by contacting the employer periodically. At any time after your interview you can write follow-up letters commenting on issues that came up in the interview, or you can forward a relevant newspaper article, another reference, or just a restatement of your interest in the position.

After your interview, you should send something to the employer every three to five days. It can be almost anything—you just want to keep your name in the decision-maker's mind until the hiring process is complete.

Even if you never do get an interview, you can still send a continuing interest letter. Don't assume that you are no longer under consideration; some employers take weeks or even months to finally hire someone. These letters are especially apropos when an employer isn't returning your calls or if for any reason you cannot call her. You need to remind that employer of your candidacy and your interest in the position. You have nothing to lose.

Continuing interest letters don't need to say much to work. In the event that an employer is frustrated with all the leading candidates, which often happens, almost any continuing interest letter can win another review of your candidacy, even if you were passed over once.

Some people who aren't even job-hunting send out an occasional continuing interest letter like the following:

> Martha, I remain quite interested in Igloo Industries, and should a sales manager position open up again, I would like you to think of me. You can reach me at work at (212) 555-1234 and at home at (212) 555-1038.

Go for It

Take a look at the following examples. The first one is for an active search; the second one for reactivating a long-dormant candidacy. Good luck!

Patrick S. Kleinen
301 Bombay Street
Kill Devil Hills, SC 28266
(803) 555-6793

February 25, 1994

D. Asher
Box #3218 (1/16/95)
c/o San Francisco Newspapers
P.O. Box 2444
San Francisco, California 94102

Dear D. Asher:

This letter follows up my application for the position of Résumé Writer.

Please know that I remain quite interested in this opportunity and am eager to discuss this position in person. I feel a one-on-one meeting will answer any questions you may have about me.

As stated in my résumé, I am experienced in a wide array of business responsibilities from advertising copywriting to marketing and sales. I feel that with my business skills as developed as they are, I am prepared to move on and up to your company. Should you need another copy of my original letter and résumé, I would be more than happy to fax them to you immediately upon your request.

I thank you for your attention to this matter and look forward to speaking with you soon.

Sincerely,

Patrick S. Kleinen

TRENT REZNOR

2311 S. Mesa Street
Phoenix, Arizona 85012

Office: (602) 555-0550
Residence: (602) 555-6931

September 5, 1994

Attn: Mr. Henry Rollins
Regional Sales Manager
U.S. West Directory
423 Palos Verdes Avenue
Phoenix, Arizona 85122

Dear Mr. Rollins:

I was quite happy that you remember my candidacy from a couple of years ago. As we discussed on the telephone, I scored in the top competitive level, had two successful and highly positive interviews, and then was out of town on business when the personnel office called me to schedule the role-playing session. (By the way, I have since talked to two friends who speak highly of you, Al Jorgenson and Paul Barker.)

I am still quite interested in U.S. West directory advertising sales. I have enclosed a copy of my updated résumé for your review. As you can see, since I last contacted Southwestern Bell I have continued to advance my career, becoming the top performer in my company. I believe the skills I have demonstrated in the past, including very strong success in directory advertising sales, would allow me to excel on behalf of your sales organization.

I am very well trained in closing major agreements with the minimum number of on-site visits. I can come up with a very large volume of advertising ideas to generate client excitement. Most important of all, I understand the needs and concerns of business people and can motivate the owners of a small take-out restaurant just as easily as I can the co-op advertising manager for a regional franchise group.

I think you can see my potential for success with your product. Under separate cover I have written to Ms. Begay in Tucson to reopen contact with her office. Would you do me the favor of putting in a good word for me with her? Your interest in my candidacy could be the key, and I am eager to explore the potential for success together.

Thank you for your help, and I'll be calling you soon with a progress report.

Sincerely,

Trent Reznor

Trent Reznor

Enclosure

Chapter Twelve
Letters for Declining an Offer

Learn to Decline Gracefully

You should be evaluating potential employers just as closely as they are evaluating you. Do they offer the opportunity you need? Is the salary package competitive? Will your coworkers be friends or fiends? Is the company really solvent, committed to this market direction, stable? If an offer is not right for you, decline it and keep looking.

Still, you may find yourself in the sensitive position of being offered a position you don't want. You must, in fact, reject all the people you have met and the company that employs them. Give a graceful reason if you want, or simply say the opportunity doesn't seem right for you at this time.

Thank everybody for their time, and keep a window open for future collaboration or communication. Most industries are like small towns, and stepping on any toes may come back to haunt you when you least expect it. Be nice to everybody. It doesn't cost much, and it can pay off big. One candidate I worked with pursued an engineering position all the way to the final job offer. He even thought the salary offer was palatable, but in the end, he decided he was overqualified for the work itself.

He declined gracefully, letting everyone he had met with know that he really appreciated being considered, but he just had to find a position more commensurate with his abilities. He was still looking four months later when they called him back and offered him a spot as a department head. He took it, skipping two levels of management and practically doubling the compensation package they had originally talked about.

Don't write that you're "declining" the offer; say that you are just "unable to accept." If you can recommend anyone else for the position, you will gracefully deflect any disappointment they may feel.

Remember, every person you meet in your job search becomes a networking contact. Your most valuable networking contacts are the people who chose you as the finalist for a position. Don't burn them.

Go for It

Take a look at the following example, and good luck!

Margaret L. Rothstein
512 Chesapeake Street, #12
Norfolk, Virginia 23711
(804) 555-5543

December 10, 1994

Robert Spitz, Executive Director
Association for Social Solutions
937 W. H Street
Washington, D.C. 20007

Dear Mr. Spitz & Members of the Hiring Committee:

Thank you for your kind offer of the position of Director of Member Relations for the Association. Unfortunately, after careful deliberation and discussion with my family, I feel that I am unable to accept. I have decided I must continue to pursue a position that more closely mirrors my future goals, and that involves a larger technology management role. Should you hear of any association planning to install a full multimedia program, please let me know immediately.

It was a pleasure to meet all of you. I am most certain of your success, and want to personally wish you all a prosperous 1995. I will continue to be interested in your progress and will assist that progress whenever you may need either my skills or position to assist you.

Finally, I took the liberty of discussing the position with Leslie Bauer, a woman of many talents, most especially concerning communications management, database systems, and direct mail. Her number is (202) 555-6311, and I gave her your number as well.

Once again, thank you for the consideration.

Best regards,

Margaret L. Rothstein

Margaret L. Rothstein

Chapter Fourteen
Letters for Accepting an Offer

The Simple Letter of Acceptance

If you simply want to document your acceptance of a job offer, a letter like this is all you need:

> Dear Hiring Authority:
>
> I am pleased to accept your offer of the position of Marketing Analyst II at a monthly salary of $3208 for the first 90 days, with a guaranteed raise to $3625 per month after the 90-day probationary period is complete. I understand that my incept date is July 1, 1994, and I am to report to Kathy Priola at 8:45 A.M. on that date. I am excited by this opportunity, and I look forward to contributing to the success of Stan & Ollie Productions, Inc.
>
> Sincerely,
>
> Your Namehere
>
> cc: Kathy Priola

At the management level, however, hiring agreements can be too complex to leave to such a simple letter of acceptance. Consider the following scenario.

Define Your Terms!

You are in a hiring meeting with the department head, the HR director, and the CFO. You're excited because you want this job, and it looks like you are about to nail it down. The hiring authority is excited because he wants you for the job as bad as you want it. The air's a little muggy. The CFO has been playing "bad cop," contesting every point of your salary, contingency, and perk demands. The HR manager is new and doesn't have answers to several of your questions. You're tired, they're tired, but you finally negotiate the offer.

Ask for a sheet of company stationery and write the deal down. Handwrite the darn thing to keep the stress level to a minimum. Title the page, AGREEMENT—OFFER TO HIRE, date it, and write down everything you've talked about. Finally, write "accepted by the candidate" and sign it; add "accepted by the company," and get as many people in the room to sign this document as you can. Congratulations, you've got a contract, about as valid as any contract is in this litigious society of ours.

Now picture this scene another way. You've negotiated the deal. Everyone is tired, but relieved. You say, "I'll need a contract, of course." The CFO has a coughing fit. The hiring manager visibly sags. "I'll have to run this through legal," says the HR director. After another week's delay you get a call. Legal says you have to renegotiate the whole thing.

Always try to get a simple agreement from every employer—dated, signed, and on company stationery—before leaving any meeting in which you negotiate a job offer. Perhaps your agreement will be quite simple, and there is no reason to complicate it, but contemporary employment agreements can be fairly complex. An executive package may involve cash salary, profit-sharing, one or more subsidized stock programs, signing and incentive bonuses, club fees, moving expenses, subsidized childcare, paid education, car and travel allowances, a shower in the office, practically anything you can imagine. Incidentally, employers have grown so heartless in discharging management-level employees that any wise manager pushes hard for a vicious penalty clause covering any termination that is not the fault of the employee. Protect yourself, or you'll have no protection at all.

As yet another safeguard, reiterate all these terms in your letter of acceptance. This will avert misunderstandings, at least. It's simple to put everything in writing at the time you're hired and can be worth a fortune later.

(Of course, this book does not purport to offer legal advice. If you have questions about employment law in your state, call a licensed attorney.)

Countering Their Offer

If you have an employment offer and you want to counter it, you can use a counter offer letter. The second letter following is an example of a counter offer.

Go for It

Take a look at the following examples, and good luck!

Carol Channeling
P.O. Box 429360
St. Louis, Missouri 63166
(314) 555-2893

October 12, 1994

Sent via fax; hard copy to follow by mail

Attn: Marvin Gunderman
VP Sales & Marketing
Conceptual Toys/Space in Action
2800 Michigan Avenue, 16th Floor
Chicago, Illinois 60610
(312) 555-2000

Dear Mr. Gunderman:

This is to confirm the terms we agreed to in our meeting of yesterday. I have accepted your offer of employment, to begin on November 14, 1994, at 9:00 A.M., with the title of Export Manager. My duties will be as stated on the job description which you gave to me yesterday. One secretary/clerk will be assigned to me full-time. My base salary will be $55,000, with a $5000 signing bonus taking effect immediately upon 90 days in service. My relocation expenses will be documented and paid by me and will be reimbursed immediately upon 90 days in service, subject to a $6,000 cap.

My basic assignment is to create at least $1,000,000 in export sales within one year. If I meet this objective within 90 days, I will earn a $5000 bonus; if I meet it within six months, I will receive a $2000 bonus. If I am on schedule to meet this goal, and I am terminated for any reason except gross insubordination, then I will receive full salary until my one-year anniversary date, or for 90 days, whichever is longer.

I have given notice at my current employer as of 9:00 A.M. this morning and have negotiated a final date of Friday, November 11, 1994, as anticipated. You may now call my immediate supervisor, Mr. Gerald Westin, at 314-555-2038 or the CFO, Ms. Holly Tarpien, at 314-555-2045. As it states in my agreement, I will have satisfied the final reference and background check unless you notify me otherwise in the next 72 hours. I expect you will like what you hear about me.

Should there be any misstatement in this letter concerning the terms we discussed, please notify me in writing immediately.

Marvin, I couldn't be happier about this. I think this is only the beginning of a long and mutually beneficial relationship. Thank you for the opportunity.

Sincerely,

Carol Channeling

Carol Channeling

PS: I've already sketched out the marketing plan. I'll have it on your desk my first day.

cc: Wally English, Human Resources, Conceptual Toys

Rima M. Suki

1501 Hiaisen Drive
Key West, Florida 33406

Residence/Message:
(305) 555-9155

MEMO

Date: April 26, 1994

Attn: Kevin Barron, CEO
Willis Community Hospital

Re: your telephone offer of yesterday

Dear Kevin:

This memo is to confirm my interest in your offer of yesterday to join Willis Community Hospital as Executive Director of Managed Care. I was very excited by the opportunity when we met in Rosslin earlier this month, and I felt we had an excellent synergy on your vision for the hospital, the new program, the medical staff, and basically everything.

Although I do have other opportunities pending, I really want to come to Rosslin and work on this project with you. If we can work out a few details, and they really are rather minor, then we can come to an agreement on this very quickly.

1. After meeting with my accountant and computing your offer several different ways, I would be more comfortable if you could raise the base to $65,000. This may seem like a small difference, but it is important to me.

2. To close out housing liabilities here, as we discussed yesterday, I would need a relocation allowance of $8,200 with no restrictions. As a related matter, your offer to pay the security deposit on a rental is most gracious, and should I not be able to find a place to buy in time, it will be appreciated.

3. The first-year bonus of $12,000 is sufficient, and I propose to structure it thus: $3000 at sign-off of business and development plan by the executive team, $3000 after acceptance of the structure and governance by the targeted providers, $3000 upon signage of the first large contract ("large contract" to be determined by mutual agreement between us), $3000 upon my anniversary.

Kevin, I believe that the united support services concept is vital in what we are planning to implement at the hospital, and I urge you to consider creating a special team bonus of 25¢ per capitated member per month to foster teamwork on all fronts from all employees of the hospital. We can discuss this further later, but we need real "buy in" from every employee from the receptionist to the top of the team, and it seems that a shared bonus will let everyone know that how they treat every one of these members is important—it will help us communicate how important it is to keep members committed to our system.

Kevin Barron, CEO
April 26, 1994, page 2

Finally, I believe it is imperative to have a systems person on our team who understands managed care capitation, who can provide full management information data when we need it and how we need it. I would be happy to provide direction to development, but I would prefer not to have to start from scratch with someone who has no prior managed care medical experience. I know someone who would be ideal, but this also is something we can discuss later.

This is the offer that makes sense to me. If you can accept this offer, I can be available at 8:00 A.M. on June 15. I am eager to begin. Please respond at your earliest opportunity.

Yours sincerely,

Rima M. Suki

Via fax; hard copy to follow by mail.

Chapter Fifteen
Letters Announcing Your New Position

Good Etiquette and Wise Planning

No matter how reclusive you usually are, conducting a full-scale job-search campaign puts you in contact with dozens and probably hundreds of people. These people take time out of their lives to help, they think about your job search, forward leads to you, talk to you on the phone, give you advice and counsel, answer your questions, meet you for interviews, and commiserate with you over lunch.

These people deserve to be notified of your success. Each and every person who assisted you in your search in the smallest manner should receive notice of your placement. This basic courtesy lets them know that they can quit worrying about you and sending you hot leads and tips, and it thanks them for their consideration. It's good manners.

Above and beyond that, however, it is also good planning. In today's relentlessly volatile job market, there is no such thing as a permanent position and little in the way of job security. No matter how good you are at your new job, you could still find yourself back out on the street due to forces entirely outside your control. If you treat your contacts with courtesy now, you will be able to count on them the next time you need them.

When to Send the Announcement

You want your announcements to go out sometime in your first two weeks in your new position. Do not send any announcement until you have actually started your new job. Ideally, you should wait until you have your new business cards, but that can sometimes take over a month.

I hate to say it, but the reason for waiting until you actually start your new job is to make sure you really have it. I've known candidates who showed up for their first day of work, only to find out the person who hired them had been laid off; they were "unhired" on the spot. The last thing you want is to announce a placement and then find yourself back on the job market, with your network ripped out from under you by the premature announcement. (See "Hiring Stories from Hell," pp. 104-105, in *The Overnight Job Change Strategy* for more disasters and more advice on how you can avoid being a victim.)

Finally, be sure to offer assistance to those who have helped you. Don't forget how nervous you felt when you called someone for basic assistance during your job search. Don't forget how thankful you were to get good sound information from someone, especially when you knew they were important and busy.

This doesn't mean you have to set up a cottage industry mentoring the careers of friends and acquaintances, but it does mean that you should return people's phone calls, if for no other reason to tell them that you can't think of any ideas, leads, or referrals that would benefit them.

Go for It

Take a look at the following example, and good luck!

CLINICAL ADVOCACY ASSOCIATES

MORS LANE AT THANATOS PARK • HIGHLAND PARK, NEW JERSEY 08904 • (310) 555-3427

Lauren A. Peabody, R.N., L.C.S.W.

December 11, 1994

Hagit Glickman, M.D., Ph.D.
Chief of Psychiatry
Park Palisades Hospital
13 River Valley View Way
Park Palisades, New Jersey 08911

Dear Dr. Glickman:

What a pleasure it was to meet with you last month. I want to thank you again for your assistance, advice, and counsel.

I am happy to announce that I have already obtained a position, thanks in part to your referral to Dr. Romanowsky at Hillside Hospital. I have accepted the position of Project Director for Clinical Advocacy Associates, a lobbying group recently formed to monitor state and federal legislation and protect the interests of mental-health professionals in the state of New Jersey. Dr. Romanowsky is a member of the group, and with his referral, I was able to meet with the Director.

This is a position with tremendous potential for me, and is an excellent segue into future nonclinical roles.

Dr. Glickman, if there is any way I can return the favor, please feel free to call on me. If there is any service I can provide on your behalf, either personally or through my position, you can count on me. (I've already put your name on CAA's mailing list.)

Once again, thank you for meeting with me, and thank you for your confidence and support.

Best regards,

Lauren A. Peabody RN, LCSW.

Lauren A. Peabody, R.N., L.C.S.W.

Chapter Sixteen
Letters of Resignation

Always Write a Letter of Resignation

You always want to document your resignation so as to reduce the potential for misunderstanding, achieve closure with your employer, and create a paper trail that can protect you later. Deliver the letter the same day you announce your impending departure.

One of my clients gave more than sufficient notice when she left an employer, but when this employer was called for a reference later, he said she quit abruptly. Since she didn't have a letter of resignation to cite, the hiring authority decided to believe her old employer. Even though she had been more than honorable, she couldn't prove it. She was passed over for the job offer.

Although there is no hard-and-fast rule, a month or more of notice is preferred at the senior management level, two weeks to a month for middle management, and a week is the absolute minimum even for the lowliest peon. Be aware that some companies immediately fire employees who quit if they are in sensitive positions. You could find yourself with an unexpected vacation if you don't know of this practice.

Be sure to date your letter of resignation, and state precisely what will be your last day. Praise the company you are leaving and thank them for the opportunities they afforded you. If there are bitter feelings, this is not the time to rub salt in old wounds. You're outa there, so don't sweat it. Good public relations never hurt anyone.

Go for It

Take a look at the following examples. A memo-style letter is just fine. Good luck!

Marcie Keeper
2826 Ramona Circle
Santa Maria, Texas 78701
915-555-2192

March 28, 1994

Roberta Jackson-Lewis
Chief, Procurement
Bartolo Engineering, Inc.
242 Watertower Road
Santa Maria, Texas 78722
915-555-3216

Dear Roberta:

Please accept this letter as formal notification of my resignation. I've greatly enjoyed my association with Bartolo Engineering and appreciate the tremendous amount I've learned from you, my associates, and our clients.

Having received a very attractive offer from a firm in Baton Rouge that will allow me to further broaden my background, I have decided that this is an appropriate time to make the leap. Certainly, without what I've gained via my association with Bartolo, this move would not be possible for me.

Because of the pressing needs of the new firm, and considering my light load of responsibilities here since the El Dorado contract fell through, my last day will be in two weeks, Friday, April 8, 1994. At that point, I will have finished the report on the Aransas Pass project and completed the first draft of the proposal for the Morgan City viaducts. Also, I have been cross-training Kyle in my duties, and I think you will find that he can easily cover my function until the Morgan City project starts to heat up.

I wish you and my associates the continued success you all deserve. I'm confident that, due to the staff's commitment to excellence and the firm's longstanding reputation, you will prosper. In the future, should I ever be able to assist the firm or you personally in any matter, please feel free to call.

Sincerely,

Marcie Keeper

Marcie Keeper

cc: Human Resources

From: Ronald Glaston
       4800 - 21st Street, Apt. 2G
       New York, New York 10010

To: Michelle Olivetti, DCM
       Rickie Ribera, CSM
       Arsenio Owlen, Supervisor
       Mason Street Claims Office
       AKA Auto Insurance Company, Inc.

CC: Personnel Office

Date: May 29, 1994

Attn: Please accept this memo as formal notice of my resignation effective in fifteen days. Wednesday, June 8, 1994, will be my last day.

I want to take the occasion in this letter to thank each of you personally for contributing to the workplace I have experienced here at AKA.

Although it has been gratifying to be the top producer in my department, and I have taken pride in my work, unfortunately the time has come for me to go on to other opportunities.

AKA afforded me the chance to learn about my own commitment to my work life and career. I have learned a great deal about producing work under pressure and about dealing with all different types of people. It has been quite an experience!

Thank you for the opportunity to serve AKA and its insureds.

Sincerely,

Ronald Glaston

Ronald C. Glaston

This employee hated this company and this job, so he wrote this wonderfully double-edged resignation.

BIBLIOGRAPHY

Many excellent quality books disappear from bookshelves before they are even remotely obsolete. I'd like you to know the publishers' toll-free order numbers so that you can order them direct if you have to. Try your local bookseller or library, but if you have trouble finding one of these titles, just call the "800" number listed after the publisher's name.

More good books on cover letters:

- *200 Letters for Job-Hunters* (revised). William Frank. Berkeley: Ten Speed Press, 1993. 800-841-BOOK.
- *Dynamic Cover Letters*. Katherine Hansen. Berkeley: Ten Speed Press, 1990. 800-841-BOOK.

Good books on résumés:

- *The Overnight Résumé*. Donald Asher. Berkeley: Ten Speed Press, 1991. 800-841-BOOK.
- *From College to Career: Entry-Level Résumés for Any Major*. Donald Asher. Berkeley: Ten Speed Press, 1992. 800-841-BOOK.
- *The Damn Good Resume Guide*, revised. Yana Parker. Berkeley: Ten Speed Press, 1989. 800-841-BOOK.
- *Designing Creative Résumés*. Gregg Berryman. Los Altos, CA: Crisp Publications, Inc., 1991. 800-442-7477.
- *The Edge Resume & Job Search Strategy*. Bill Corbin and Shelbi Wright. Carmel, IN: UN Communications, Inc., 1993. 800-434-EDGE.

The best book ever on careers and career decision-making:

- *The 1994 What Color is Your Parachute? A practical manual for job-hunters and career-changers*. Richard Nelson Bolles. Berkeley: Ten Speed Press, 1993. 800-841-BOOK.

Two awfully good books on job-search strategies and techniques:

- *The Overnight Job Change Strategy*. Donald Asher. Berkeley: Ten Speed Press, 1993. 800-841-BOOK.
- *Who's Hiring Who?* Richard Lathrop. Berkeley: Ten Speed Press, 1989. 800-841-BOOK.

Good books on interviewing and salary negotiations:

- *Sweaty Palms: The Neglected Art of Being Interviewed* (rev.). H. Anthony Medley. Berkeley: Ten Speed Press, 1992. 800-841-BOOK.
- *Information Interviewing: What It Is and How to Use It in Your Career*. Martha Stoodley. Garrett Park, MD: Garrett Park Press, 1990. 301-946-2553.
- *Knock 'Em Dead: With Great Answers to Tough Interview Questions*. Martin J. Yate. Boston: Bob Adams, 1990. 800-872-5627.
- *How to Make $1000 a Minute: Negotiating Salaries & Raises*. Jack Chapman. Berkeley: Ten Speed Press, 1987. 800-841-BOOK.
- *The First Five Minutes: The Successful Opening Moves in Business, Sales & Interviews*. N. King. New York: Prentice-Hall, 1989. 800-223-2336.

Good books on headhunters and how to use them:

- *Rites of Passage at $100,000+: The Insider's Guide to Absolutely Everything about Executive Job-Changing.* John Lucht. New York: Henry Holt & Co., 1988. 800-CALL-WILEY.

- *The Headhunter Strategy: How to Make It Work for You.* Ken Cole. New York: John Wiley & Sons, 1985. 800-841-BOOK.

- *The Directory of Executive Recruiters.* Fitzwilliam, New Hamp.: Kennedy Publications, annual. 603-585-2200 or 603-585-6544.

- *The Recruiting & Search Report* (a database service). Panama City Beach, Fl.: K. Cole & Co. 904-235-3733 or 800-634-4548.

Exercises and Sample Letters

Exercises and Sample Letters

Exercises and Sample Letters

Also by Donald Asher:

The Overnight Résumé

The companion to this book shows how to put together a hard-hitting, professional résumé for any field, in just one night if need be. $7.95, 136 pages

The Overnight Job Change Strategy

Fast, effective job-search strategies, including how to identify the companies that need you, get an interview, and win a great job—even when your target company isn't hiring. $7.95, 136 pages

From College to Career

Specifically tailored to college students, these entry-level résumés illustrate how to present any academic or job experience (or lack thereof) in the best possible light. $7.95, 128 pages

. . . . And More Help for the Job Hunter

What Color Is Your Parachute? by Richard N. Bolles

This best-selling classic is substantially revised and updated every year. Practical advice, step-by-step exercises, and a warm, human tone make it *the* guide for job-hunters and career-changers. "The giant title in the field."—*The New York Times* $14.95, 488 pages

200 Letters for Job Hunters by William S. Frank

The complete letter-writing reference, with a wealth of real-life examples covering everything from initial networking to the final follow-up. Newly revised to be even more effective. $17.95, 352 pages

Sweaty Palms by H. Anthony Medley

One of the most popular books ever on job interviewing is now fully revised and updated for the 90s. Tells how to prepare for an interview, answer even the most difficult questions, and leave a great impression. $9.95, 194 pages

✿

Available at your local bookstore, or order direct from the publisher. Please include $3.50 shipping and handling for the first book, and 50 cents for each additional book. California residents include local sales tax. For VISA, Mastercard, or American Express orders, call (800) 841-BOOK. Write for our free catalog of over 500 books and tapes.

Ten Speed Press
Post Office Box 7123
Berkeley, California 94707
(800) 841-BOOK